nglish for
rmation Technology

1

Vocational English
Course Book

Maja Olejniczak

Series editor David Bonamy

Contents

1 Working in the IT industry

- introduce yourself and others
- ask and answer personal questions
- talk about scheduled tasks
- use the alphabet and spell out words

Meeting people

Speaking **1** How do you greet people in your country? What do you say when you greet people in English?

Reading **2** Complete these dialogues with the words in the box.

all	is	meet	name's	Nice	this
too	you	Welcome	What's		

1 Natasha: Hi, my (1) _____ Natasha.
   Khalid: Pleased to (2) _____ you. I'm Khalid Ali.
   Natasha: Pleased to meet you, (3) _____ .

2 Philip: Good morning. (4) _____ your name?
   Ahmed: I'm Ahmed. And (5) _____ are?
   Philip: My name's Philip. (6) _____ to meet you.

3 Tim: Hi everybody, (7) _____ is Ingrid.
   All: Hi!
   Tim: Ingrid, this (8) _____ Ahmed, Linda, Mohammed and Mansoor.
   Ingrid: Nice meeting you (9) _____ .
   Linda: Likewise.
   Tim: (10) _____ to the team and good luck.

Listening **3** 🎧 2 Listen and check your answers.

4 Listen again and repeat the dialogues.

Speaking **5** Work in small groups. Practise introductions. Follow the instructions below.
   1 Introduce yourself.
   2 Introduce a new team member.

Listening **6** 🎧 **3** Listen to this dialogue and choose the correct answers.

Kathryn: Karim, what do you do?
Karim: I'm a (1) *website developer/network administrator*. Who do you work for?
Kathryn: I work for CISCO. I'm a (2) *system analyst/website analyst* there. Where are you from, Karim?
Karim: I'm from Kuwait. I work for Microsoft there. And where are you from, Kathryn?
Kathryn: I'm from the (3) *UK/US* but now I live in Qatar. Do you know where Glenda's from?
Karim: She's from the US.
Kathryn: And what's her job?
Karim: She works for (4) *IBM/Dell*. Her job is to set up new systems.

Language

Present tense of *be*

We use *be* to say who somebody is or what something is.	*I'm Sam.*	*I am Sam.*
	You're/We're/They're from the UK.	*You/ We/They are from the UK.*
	He's/She's a website developer.	*He/She is a website developer.*
	It's in the US.	*It is in the US.*
We use *be* to ask personal questions.	*Where are you from?*	
	What's his name/job?	*What is his name/job?*

Listening **7** 🎧 **4** Listen and repeat these words.

I'm, You're, She's, He's, It's, We're, They're/Their

Reading **8** Complete this email with *am*, *is*, *are*, *their*, *our* or *my*.

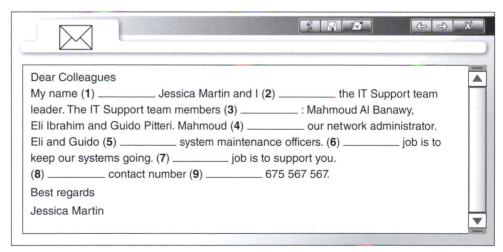

Dear Colleagues
My name (**1**) _____ Jessica Martin and I (**2**) _____ the IT Support team leader. The IT Support team members (**3**) _____ : Mahmoud Al Banawy, Eli Ibrahim and Guido Pitteri. Mahmoud (**4**) _____ our network administrator. Eli and Guido (**5**) _____ system maintenance officers. (**6**) _____ job is to keep our systems going. (**7**) _____ job is to support you.
(**8**) _____ contact number (**9**) _____ 675 567 567.

Best regards

Jessica Martin

Writing **9** Write a reply to the email in 8. Introduce yourself and three people in your group.

Speaking **10** Work in pairs. Ask and answer questions about your jobs, companies and nationalities.

Example:
A: *Where are you from?*
B: *I'm from … .*

Jobs in IT

Speaking **1** Work in small groups. List the IT jobs you know.

Reading **2** Read this team introduction. Complete the descriptions 1–4 with the IT jobs in the box.

> Hi! I'm Sylvia. I create usernames and passwords and I set firewalls.
> This is Isabelle. Her job is to plan and design the network. And this is Andrew. His job is to make sure all of the computers work properly. Finally, Mark and Latika. Their area is data processing. We all work for the university. Our offices are in building 8.

database analyst(s)	IT support officer(s)	network administrator(s)
network architect(s)		

1 Sylvia is a _____ .
2 Isabelle is a _____ .
3 Andrew is an _____ .
4 Mark and Latika are _____ .

Language

Present simple

We use the **present simple** to talk about routines and things that are permanent or happen all the time.	*What **do** you **do**? I'm a programmer.*
	*What **does** she **do**? She's a developer.*
	*Where **does** she **work**? She **works** for IBM in Poland. She **doesn't work** in Estonia.*
	*Where **do** they **work**? They **work** for Siemens in Egypt.*
	***Do** you **work** in IT? Yes, I **do**/No I **don't**.*

Listening **3** 🔲 **5** Listen to three people talking about their jobs. Complete these job descriptions.

1 Karl
 Job: software _____
 Responsibilities: he designs and _____ computer games.
2 Heba
 Job: _____ analyst
 Responsibilities: he _____ computer problems.
3 Wojtek
 Job: database _____
 Responsibilities: he analyses and _____ electronic data.

Speaking   **4**   Work in pairs. Ask and answer questions about Karl, Heba and Wojtek.

Example:
A: What does Karl do?
B: He's ... .

Listening   **5**   ▶ 🎧 6   Listen and complete this dialogue.

Ahmed: Where (1) _____ you work, Betty?
Betty: I work for Dell in Dubai. What (2) _____ you?
Ahmed: I (3) _____ for HP in Budapest. What do you (4) _____ , Milo?
Milo: I'm a (5) _____ developer. I work (6) _____ Microsoft in Prague.
Betty: Milo, do you (7) _____ Frida?
Milo: Yes, I do. What do you (8) _____ to know?
Betty: Where (9) _____ she work?
Milo: She works with (10) _____ in Prague. She designs websites for
           (11) _____ .
Ahmed: I see. Right, let's go. The workshop starts in five minutes.

6   ▶ 🎧 7   Listen and repeat these questions.

1   Where do you work?
2   What about you?
3   What do you do?
4   What do you want to know?
5   Where does she work?

Writing   **7**   What is your dream job? Write a job description for the job of your choice.

Job:

Company to work for:

Responsibilities:

Speaking   **8**   Tell the rest of the group about your dream job. Use your notes to help you.
Example: My dream job is ... . I design/solve/analyse ... .

Schedules

Listening **1** 📀 8 Listen to two people at an IT conference. Complete this dialogue.

Penelope:	Hi, Don. (1) _____ are you?
Don:	I'm (2) _____ thanks, Penelope. And you?
Penelope:	I'm OK. Bit tired from the flight.
Don:	Right.
Penelope:	(3) _____ workshop (4) _____ you want to attend today, Don?
Don:	I want to go to the CISCO network security workshop.
Penelope:	Sounds interesting. What time does it start?
Don:	It (5) _____ at 9.15.
Penelope:	And (6) _____ does it finish?
Don:	It (7) _____ at 4.00 in the afternoon.
Penelope:	Well, I (8) _____ to attend the Microsoft Windows Applications workshop. It (9) _____ at 8.30 am and (10) _____ at 6.00 pm. But they have two breaks, at 10.30 and 12.45.
Don:	That's good.
Penelope:	Hope you enjoy your session.
Don:	You too. See you around.

Language

Schedules
We use *at* with clock times.

	It **starts at** 9.15. (nine fifteen/quarter past nine)
	It **begins at** 8.30. (eight thirty/half past eight)
What time does it start/begin/finish/end?	It **finishes at** 4.00. (four o'clock)
	It **ends at** 5.05. (five oh five/five past five)
When do you have a break?	We **have a break at** 12.45. (twelve forty-five/a quarter to one)

Listening **2** 📀 9 Listen and repeat these times.

1	7.05		5	4.35
2	6.45		6	2.15
3	8 o'clock		7	12 o'clock
4	10.45		8	9.50

3 🔊 **10** Listen and repeat these sentences.

1 It finishes at 5.00.
2 It ends at 8.00.
3 It starts at 6.00.

Speaking **4** Work in pairs. Ask and answer questions about your daily schedule and breaks. Make notes.

Example:
A: What time/When do you start work?
B: I start at 8.00. What about you?
A: I begin at … .

5 Tell another pair about your partner's schedule.

Example: … starts work at 8.00 and finishes at 4.00. She has a break at 12.00.

Reading **6** Complete these sentences with the words in the box.

at	at	in	for	from

I work in an office (1) _____ Dubai but I'm (2) _____ Canada. I work
(3) _____ SAP there. I start work (4) _____ 8.15, have lunch in a café
(5) _____ 1.30 and finish about 5.00.

Writing **7** Write three sentences about yourself and your daily schedule.

Spelling

Speaking **1** Work in small groups. List the IT acronyms you know.

> **HTML** (HyperText Markup Language) HTML is a mark-up language used to describe the structure of a web page.

> **FTP** (File Transfer Protocol) a standard network protocol used to copy a file from one host to another.

> **WLAN** (Wireless Local Area Network) A type of local-area network that uses high-frequency radio wires to communicate between nodes.

Listening **2** 🔵 11 Listen and complete this dialogue.

Andrei: Bob, can you (1) _____ me, please?
Bob: Sure.
Andrei: I don't understand this acronym. What does it (2) _____ for?
Bob: Let me see. 'W3'. I'm not sure. Maybe WWW, the World Wide Web.
Andrei: OK. What does P2P stand for?
Bob: (3) _____ stands for person-to-person.
Andrei: OK. What does IP (4) _____?
Bob: It means Internet Protocol.
Andrei: How do you (5) _____ 'Protocol'?
Bob: p – r – o – t – o – c – o – l.
Andrei: Thanks.
Bob: You're welcome.

3 🔵 12 Listen to the letters and repeat them.

a h j k
b c d e g p t v z
f l m n s x z
i y
o
q u w
r

> Z /zed/ in British English and /zee/ in American English.

Speaking **4** Work in pairs. Make a list of acronyms. Ask and answer questions.

Example:
A: *What does HTML stand for/mean?*
B: *It stands for/means ... .*

Business matters

Writing **1** You are at a training workshop. The trainer asks all the trainees to complete the form and introduce themselves. Complete this form about yourself.

Participant Information

Name: _____ Date: _____

DOB: _____ Place of residence: _____

Contact: Phone _____ Email _____

Interests: _____

_____

IT job you want and why: _____

_____

_____

_____

_____

_____

---

2 Work in pairs. Swap your profiles and introduce your partner.

3 Write an email message to introduce yourself to the employees in the company using the profile below or your own information.

> You are a new employee in a company. Your position is a network administrator. You are responsible for setting up firewalls, security levels, wireless connection, usernames and passwords.

Speaking **4** Work in pairs. Student A: you are the IT help desk coordinator, Mrs Mahmoud. Turn to page 68. Student B: you are Sharifa. Turn to page 78. Complete the task. Swap the roles.

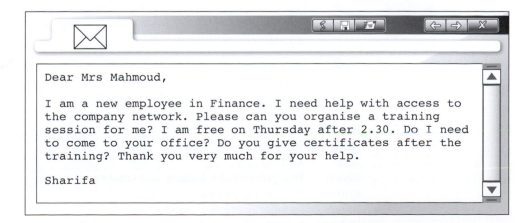

```
Dear Mrs Mahmoud,

I am a new employee in Finance. I need help with access to
the company network. Please can you organise a training
session for me? I am free on Thursday after 2.30. Do I need
to come to your office? Do you give certificates after the
training? Thank you very much for your help.

Sharifa
```

Computer systems

- make comparisons
- talk about what is happening now
- talk about ability and necessity
- talk about obligations

Computer hardware

Speaking **1** Work in small groups. Make a list of all the computer hardware you use in your work or study.

Vocabulary **2** Match the things in the diagram with the correct items 1–11.

1 monitor ☐
2 case ☐
3 motherboard ☐
4 CPU (Central Processing Unit or Processor) ☐
5 main memory (RAM) ☐
6 expansion cards (video, graphic) ☐
7 power supply unit ☐
8 optical disc drive ☐
9 hard disk drive ☐
10 keyboard ☐
11 mouse ☐

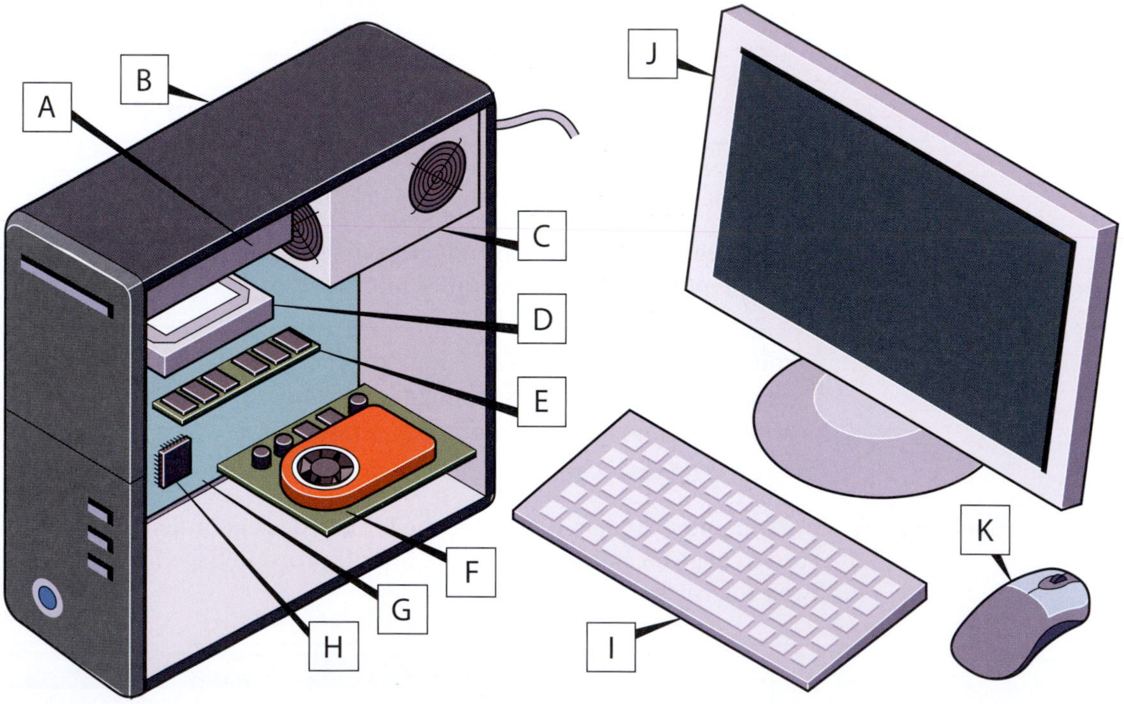

Listening **3** 🔊 13 Listen to two colleagues and complete this dialogue.

Bob: What do you think? Which (1) _____ is better for the sales team?
Daisy: I'm not sure. This computer has a (2) _____ memory and I think it has a (3) _____ processor.
Bob: And the other one?
Daisy: Well, it is (4) _____ .
Bob: And (5) _____ .
Daisy: Yes, you're right. Lighter and smaller.
Bob: But the bigger one is (6) _____ .
Daisy: So what is our decision?
Bob: I'm not sure. Let's go for a coffee and discuss this again.

Language

Comparatives			
We use comparative adjectives to compare two people or things.			

For short adjectives we add **-er (than)**. Be careful of spelling.	big	**bigger**	The new monitor was **bigger than** the old monitor.
	fast	**faster**	Your processor is **faster than** mine.
	easy	**easier**	It's **easier** to use **than** the other one.
For long adjectives we use **more/less (than)**.	difficult	**more/less difficult**	This version is **more difficult** to use **than** the old version.
	expensive	**more/less expensive**	His computer is **less expensive than** hers.
	reliable	**more/less reliable**	I think you should buy that CPU. It is **more reliable than** the one you have.
Some comparatives are irregular.	bad	**worse**	That screen resolution is much **worse** than before!
	good	**better**	I really like this mouse. It's so much **better** than the old one.

4 Make the comparative form of these adjectives.

Example: long longer

1 light _____
2 efficient _____
3 long _____
4 wide _____
5 heavy _____
6 fast _____
7 dark _____
8 soft _____
9 hard _____
10 durable _____

Listening **5** ▶ 🕐 **14** Listen and check your answers.

6 Listen again and repeat the words.

Reading **7** Read these product descriptions and make sentences using comparatives.

Example: The Corsair is longer than the Imation but slimmer.

Corsair Flash Survivor GT 8GB

8GB
Read at 34MB/s
Write at 28MB/s
3.25" x 0.75"
Aluminium
256-bit AES
SW encryption
Ten year warranty
Price £25

Imation Clip Flash Drive 4GB

4GB
Read at 15MB/s
Write at 9MB/s
2.95" x 1.14"
Plastic
No data encryption
Five year warranty
Price £10

Writing **8** Work in pairs. Write an email to a colleague comparing the two products in 7.

Computer software

Speaking **1** Work in small groups. Make a list of all the computer software you use in your work or study. Think about:

- application software
- programming software
- system software

2 Make a list of the computer software your non-IT colleagues use.

Language

Superlatives
We use superlative adjectives to compare a person or thing with a number of other people or things.

For short adjectives we add ***the + -est***. Be careful of spelling.	big	***biggest***	The new monitor was **the biggest** in the room.
	fast	***fastest***	Your version of the software is **the fastest**.
	easy	***easiest***	It's **the easiest** to use.
For long adjectives we use ***the most/the least***.	difficult	***the most/least difficult***	This version is **the most difficult** to use.
	expensive	***the most/least expensive***	His computer is **the least expensive**.
	reliable	***the most/least reliable***	I think you should buy that. It is the **most reliable**.
Some superlatives are irregular.	bad	***the worst***	That is **the worst** software I've ever used!
	good	***the best***	I really like this website. It's **the best** I've seen.

Speaking **3** Work in small groups. Talk about the software you and your non-IT colleagues use. Answer these questions.

1 What are the differences between the IT and non-IT software you have listed?
2 Which is the cheapest?
3 Which is the most expensive?
4 Which is the most/least reliable?
5 Which is the most difficult/easiest to use?
6 Which is the best/worst?
7 Which is the most/least user-friendly?

Listening **4** 🔊 **15** Listen to two colleagues discussing software and complete this dialogue.

Tim: What do you think about these three photo imaging packages?

Simone: It's a difficult choice. All three are very good but they have different strengths.

Tim: I agree.

Simone: Serif Image Plus has (1) _____ image (2) _____ .

Tim: OK.

Simone: But Magic Extreme has the (3) _____ processing of images.

Tim: You're right. Also, Serif has (4) _____ special (5) _____ . But what about Snap Pro?

Simone: Well, it has the (6) _____ dubbing options.

Tim: And Snap Pro is the best for (7) _____ photos.

Simone: I'm not sure. Serif has (8) _____ efficient (9) _____ .

Tim: Which is the most expensive?

Simone: Oh, Serif Image Plus.

Tim: And the cheapest?

Simone: Snap Pro.

Tim: Let's get Snap Pro then.

Simone: I'm still not sure!

Language

Present tense of have (got)

We use **have (got)** to talk about possession.	I've/You've/We've/They've **(got)** … | I/You/We/They **have (got)** …

I've/You've/We've/They've **(got)** …	I/You/We/They **have (got)** …
He's/She's/It's **(got)** …	He/She/It **has (got)** …
I/You/We/They **haven't (got)** …	I/You/We/They **have not (got)** …
He/She/It **hasn't (got)** …	He/She/It **has not (got)** …
I/You/We/They **don't have** …	I/You/We/They **do not have** …
He/She/It **doesn't have** …	He/She/It **does not have** …
Have I/you/we/they **got** …?	
Has he/she/it **got** …?	
Do I/you/we/they **have** …?	
Does he/she/it **have** …?	

Listening **5** 🔊 **16** Listen and repeat these sentences.

1   We've got the best software.
2   Does it have the most reliable anti-virus software?
3   She has the cheapest computer.
4   They haven't got the latest version.
5   Do you have the fastest processor?
6   Has it got Windows?
7   They have the latest software.
8   It has the biggest screen.

Writing **6** Work in pairs. Write five sentences comparing three software products you use or know.

Working with computers

Listening **1** 🔘 17 Listen and complete this dialogue.

Paul: Hi, Brinitha.
Brinitha: Hi, Paul.
Paul: How's it (1) _____ ?
Brinitha: Fine, fine.
Paul: What (2) _____ you (3) _____ at the moment?
Brinitha: Oh, I (4) _____ Nero.
Paul: How are you getting on?
Brinitha: Well, I (5) _____ a network. I (6) _____ Microsoft Server.
Paul: Right. Where is Jackie today? Do you know?
Brinitha: Yes. She is on a training course today. She (7) _____ about the new database system.
Paul: What about Mary and Imran? Where are they?
Brinitha: They (8) _____ in today. They have a day off.

Language

Present continuous

	*I'm **installing** the software.*
	*He's/She's **setting up** a network.*
	*We're/They're **working** at home today.*
	*I'm **not setting up** the network.*
We use the **present continuous** to talk about things that take place at the time of speaking and are not permanent.	*He's/She's **not installing** the software.*
	*We/They **aren't coming** in today.*
	***Are** you **installing** it now?*
	***What am** I **doing**?*
	***What are** you/they **doing**?*
	***What is** he/she **doing**?*

2 Complete these sentences with *is/isn't*, *am/am not*, *are/aren't*.

1 It _____ going well.
2 I _____ learning a new program.
3 She _____ working in the office today. She has a day off.
4 They _____ installing the new software.
5 We _____ setting up the network.
6 We _____ using Word. We have a different word-processing program.
7 Where _____ they working today?
8 What _____ he installing on the computer?
9 I _____ coming in today. I'm sick.
10 _____ she working at home today?

Vocabulary **3** Match the sentence halves 1–8 to a–h.

1 Hanka is creating   a) the software.
2 Philip is inserting an   b) a check-up.
3 Rob is troubleshooting   c) a file.
4 We are running   d) a device.
5 Betty is connecting   e) CDs.
6 They are burning   f) image.

Listening **4** ▶ 🖭 18 Listen and repeat these sentences.

1 What are you doing now?
2 Are they setting up the network?
3 She's working at home today.
4 I'm not installing the software.
5 We're not using Word.

Speaking **5** Look at the pictures A–F. Describe what is happening.

Example: He is moving …

6 Work in pairs or small groups. Talk about what you are doing at the moment in your work or study.

Writing **7** Write three sentences saying what you and your colleges are doing at the moment in your work or study.

Computer usage

1 Read what Ben says about computer usage in his office. Answer the questions.

1 What **must** Ben do?
2 What **can** Ben do?
3 What **can't** Ben do?
4 Can he open any website?
5 Why is it important to follow computer dos and don'ts?

Speaking **2** Make a list of computer usage where you work or study. Compare your list with the group.

Language

must, mustn't, can, can't, don't have to

We use **must** and **mustn't** for obligations.	You **must** come to work on time.
	You **mustn't** be late.
We use **can** and **can't** for possibility and ability.	He **can** use Word but he **can't** use Excel.
We use **have to** for something that is necessary.	I **have to** log in using my password.
We use **don't have to** for something that is not necessary.	We **don't have to** work at the weekend.

Writing **3** Write an email to a colleague about yourself using *must, mustn't, can, can't, have to, don't have to*.

Business matters

Speaking **1** A company asks you to recommend a computer and work station configuration for their sales team. In small groups, decide what to recommend. Use the office floor plan below to prepare the computer and work station configuration. Think about these things:

1. There are six people in the sales team.
2. Five people are out of the office four days of the week.
3. One person is in the office all the time – the team admin assistant.
4. Employees need a network connection (wired and wireless).
5. Employees print, scan and copy.
6. Company and client data must be stored on a separate device and backed up regularly.

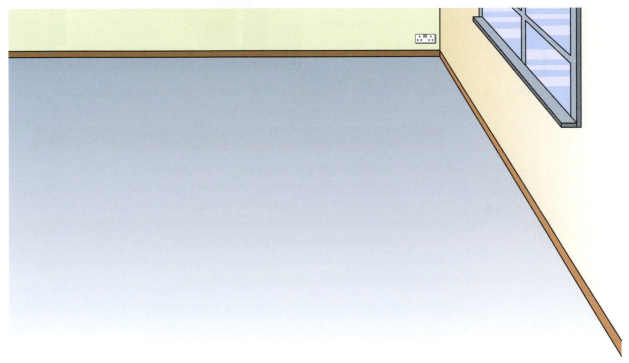

2 Make your recommendations to another group. Choose the best computer configuration.

Example: We recommend this configuration. You have … . /It has … .

Writing **3** Write a short email to the IT manager with your recommendations.

3 Websites

- discuss the purpose of websites
- talk about website features
- describe a process
- write a proposal

Website purpose

Speaking **1** Which websites do you use in your work and study? Make a list and share it with a partner. Do you use the same sites?

Reading **2** Read this text about different types of website. Answer these questions.

TYPES OF WEBSITE – A GUIDE FOR WEBSITE DESIGNERS

The purpose of an organisational website is to inform about an idea or event. Companies develop commercial websites to sell products or services. Entertainment websites are designed to entertain or provide fun activities. People visit news websites to obtain information. The purpose of a personal website is to provide information about an individual. Social networking websites help people to exchange personal information. Educational websites aim to share knowledge and enable online learning.

1 Why do people visit organisational websites?
2 Why do people visit company websites?
3 Why do people visit entertainment websites?
4 Why do people visit news websites?

Vocabulary **3** Complete these sentences about the purpose of websites with the words in the box.

| offer | practise | ~~present~~ | promote | read | sell | share |

Example: The purpose of Nationalgeographic.com is to _present_ information on topics.

1 People visit CNN.com to _____ international news.
2 Some websites want to _____ a service.
3 Companies use Amazon.com to _____ their products.
4 Thegreenshoppingguide.co.uk wants to _____ environmentally friendly shopping.
5 Students visit Math.com to _____ their maths.
6 English teachers join eltforum.com to _____ teaching resources.

Language

Question words (1)

We use **which** to ask about things. We can use it with a noun.	**Which** *websites do you visit/go to?* *I use Wikipedia a lot.*
We use **what** to ask about things.	**What** *do you use CNN for?* *I use it to get the news.*
We use **why** to ask the reason for something.	**Why** *do you use Wikipedia?* *I use Wikipedia to check information.*
We use **when** to ask about time.	**When** *do you use CNN?* *In my lunchbreak.*

Listening **4** 🌐 19 Listen and repeat these questions.

1 Which websites do you use?
2 Why do you use Wikipedia?
3 What do you use CNN for?
4 When does she use CNN?

Speaking **5** Work in pairs. Use the websites you listed in 1 to ask and answer questions.

Example:
A: Which websites do you use?
B: I use … .

6 Go around the class and ask five students to name the websites they visit and use at home. Write down a website for each of the four headings 1–4 in the table.

Interviewee name	Interviewee uses these websites to:			
	1 entertain	2 get news	3 research/study	4 shop
a)				
b)				
c)				
d)				
e)				

7 Present the information you collected to the group. Which are the most popular websites for each heading?

Website analytics

1 What information can you get about website traffic using a website analysis application? Work in pairs. Make a list.

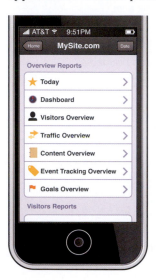

Reading **2** Which items of the analytics programme above answer these questions?

Example:
A: Where do you find information about the website's visitors?
B: In 'Visitors Overview'.

1 Where can you find out how many people visit the website?
2 Where can you see what percentage of people view only one page on the website?
3 Where do you find information about how long they spend on the website?
4 Where do you see how many people searched for 'gotapps' to find the website?

Listening **3** 🔊 **20** Listen to Sarah and George. Complete this dialogue.

Sarah: George, I (1) _____ some information about our website.
George: OK, what do you need to (2) _____ ?
Sarah: Well, I need some information about website (3) _____ , you know, external visits to our website.
George: OK.
Sarah: (4) _____ you do a report for me?
George: Sure. (5) _____ do you need it by?
Sarah: Er, tomorrow morning, I'm (6) _____ . It's for the finance director.
George: OK, what do you need to know (7) _____ ?
Sarah: Well, the (8) _____ of visitors to our website last month, their movements and actions on the website, and where they're from.
George: OK, I (9) _____ do that.
Sarah: Thanks very (10) _____ indeed.

Vocabulary **4** Match the website analysis tools 1–5 to the descriptions a–e.

1 traffic
2 meta tag
3 visitor map
4 user profile
5 page optimisation

a) information about where the visitors to your site are from
b) invisible information (e.g. a hidden keyword) on a website
c) information about a user and the sites they browse
d) increasing the number of visitors to your site
e) the movement and actions of visitors to your site

Language

Question words (2)		
We use **how much/how many** to ask about quantity.	**How many** people visit our website every day? *About 20,000.*	
	How many hits do we get each month? *About 40,000.*	
We use **where** to ask about places.	**Where** are the visitors from? *From Asia and the US.*	
	Where do they go on our website? *To 'News'.*	
We can use **how** + adjective/adverb to ask about degree.	**How often** do people visit our website? *At least once a day.*	

Listening   **5**   ▶ 🎧 **21**   Listen and repeat these questions.

1   How many people visit the site?
2   Where do they go on the website?
3   How long do they spend on the website?

Language

Large numbers	
20,000	*twenty thousand*
400,000	*four hundred thousand*
500,000	*five hundred thousand/half a million*
3,000,000	*three million*

6   How do you say these numbers?

1   30,000
2   700,000
3   10,000,000
4   100,000
5   80,000

Listening   **7**   ▶ 🎧 **22**   Listen and check your answers.

Speaking   **8**   Work in pairs. You both work in website analytics. Ask and answer questions about website visits.

Student A: Turn to page 68
Student B: Turn to page 78

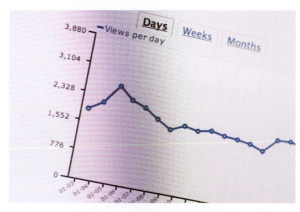

Website development

Speaking **1** Describe something you do every day at home or at work. Use the words in the Language box below.

Example: Sending an email.
First, click on 'New email'. After that … .

Language

Describing steps in a process		
We use *first*, *next*, *then*, *after that* (etc.) to describe the order of actions.	*First*, do … .	*To start*, do … .
	After that, … .	*Next*, … .
	Then, … .	
	Secondly, … .	*Thirdly*, … .
	Finally, … .	*To finish*, … .

Reading **2** Complete this text with the words in the box.

After that	Finally	First	Next	Secondly	Then	Thirdly

The steps in website development

(1) _____ , discuss with the customer their requirements and the target audience. Find out what features and number of pages they want on their site. (2) _____ , analyse the information from the customer. (3) _____ , create a website specification. (4) _____ design and develop the website. (5) _____ , assign a specialist to write the website content. (6) _____ give the project to programmers for HTML coding. (7) _____ , test the website.

After you publish the website, update and maintain it on an ongoing basis. Monitor customer use.

3 Work in pairs. Complete the flowchart to show the website development process.

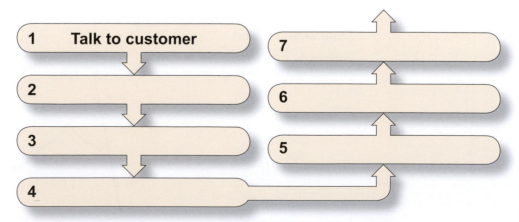

1 **Talk to customer**
2
3
4
5
6
7

Speaking **4** Describe the website development process to another pair in your own words.

Reading **5** Look at the websites below and answer these questions.

1 What are the websites?
2 Do you use these websites? Why/Why not?
3 What is the purpose of each website: sell, inform, share, educate?
4 What are the main features of each website?
5 Think of two more websites that have the same purpose. Are they different to the ones below? Why?

Writing **6** You are the owner of a company that needs a new website. Make a list of things that you need/would like for your website. Answer the following questions.

• What is the name of your company?
• What is the business type?
• What is the purpose of your website?

Speaking **7** Work in pairs. Student A is the website developer. Student B is the customer. Ask and answer questions about website requirements. Swap roles.

Example:
A: What is the name of your company?
B: It's called/Its name is … .

The best websites

Vocabulary **1** What are your favourite websites? Why? Use the words in the box to describe them.

| beautiful | well-designed | easy-to-use/navigate | clear | reliable |
| useful | informative | fun | funny | exciting | interesting |

Example: The most exciting website is … because … .

Language

Describing things

There's/There is/There isn't	**There's** a lot of information on this website.
There are/aren't	**There aren't** many photos on this website.
Has	The website **has** good graphics.
Have	Most websites **have** a lot of features.

Writing **2** Write about the things you like and dislike about different websites.

Example: I really like the look of the Nickelodeon website. It has … .

Speaking **3** What are the trends in website design? Discuss with the group.

Example: Websites use more video now.

Business matters

Reading **1** You are a website designer. Read the information about Learning Now Ltd. Answer these questions.

- What is the business type?
- What is the purpose of the website: sell, inform, share, educate?
- Who are the website users? Where are the website users?
- What are the features of the website?

Learning Now Ltd

Learning Now Ltd is in the education business. It needs a new website to promote its courses, materials and learning resources and provide online language-learning services. The website users are young adults all around the world. The website needs to have these features: good interactivity, audio and fast download times.

Writing **2** In pairs, write a proposal for Learning Now Ltd's website. Use your answers from 1 and the template below to help you.

Proposal No. 2011/32154	**Date:**
Customer:	**Business activity:**
Subject:	
Purpose:	
Users:	
Features:	
Proposal presented by:	

Speaking **3** Present your proposal to the group.

- talk about databases
- talk about data processing
- ask for and give advice
- talk about company departments

Database basics

Speaking **1** What database products do you know and use at work and at home?

Listening **2** [▶ 🌐 23] Listen to two colleagues at a book company. Chris needs some information from the production database. Complete this dialogue.

Chris: Tim, (1)_____ you help me a moment, please?

Tim: Sure. What's the (2)_____?

Chris: I need some (3)_____ about a book budget from the database.

Tim: OK.

Chris: But I don't know how to (4)_____ it.

Tim: No problem.

Chris: So what do I do first?

Tim: Enter your name and (5)_____ and press enter.

Chris: Erm … ?

Tim: You have got a password?

Chris: Erm, I can't (6)_____ it.

Tim: Use mine. Type in t evans, that's t – e – v – a – n – s, then snavet. s – n – a – v – e – t.

Chris: OK.

Tim: Now press Enter. Now what is the name of the book?

Chris: *Basic French*.

Tim: OK. Type in that in the title (7)_____ in the first (8)_____. Now press Find. There it is. OK, budget. Click (9)_____ Publishing and scroll down to Plant costs and click on that.

Chris: Good. There's the budget in the second row. Thanks, Tim.

Tim: No problem.

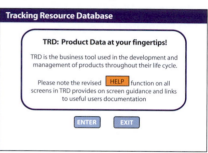

Project title	**Basic French**		
	Budget 40 000	Cost to date	Difference
Editorial	10 000	8 000	+2 000
Design	13 000	12 000	+1 000
Multimedia	5 000	0	+5 000
Freelance	7 000	1 000	+6 000
Marketing	5 000	6 000	−1 000
Summary		27 000	+13 000

Language

<table>
<tr><td colspan="2">Asking people to do things</td></tr>
<tr>
<td rowspan="6">We use can/could/would you + infinitive without to when we ask somebody to do something for us.</td>
<td>Could you help me, please?
Sure.</td>
</tr>
<tr>
<td>Please could you help?
No problem.</td>
</tr>
<tr>
<td>Can you explain what a database is, please?
I'm afraid I can't.</td>
</tr>
<tr>
<td>Please can you explain what a database is?
I'm sorry, I can't.</td>
</tr>
<tr>
<td>Would you explain that, please?
Could you come back a bit later? I'm busy right now.</td>
</tr>
</table>

Listening   **3**   ▶ 🌐 **24**   Listen and repeat these questions.

1 Could you help me, please?
2 Please could you help me?
3 Would you help me with this software?
4 Please could you explain how to do that?
5 Please would you give me your password?

Speaking   **4**   Work in pairs. Student A: make questions from the prompts. Student B: answer *yes* or *no* and give a reason why not (if your answer is no).

Example: type/name
Could you type in your name, please?

1 open/window
2 turn up/air conditioning
3 turn down/mp3 player
4 give/you/pen
5 answer/phone
6 give/password

5   Work in pairs. Use the example of a database below to explain to your partner what a database is. Use these words: *store, access, get, fields, columns, rows.*

Example: A database is used to … . This is a … .

First Name	Last Name	Department	Title	Phone ext.
John	**Smith**	Development	Engineer	123
Jane	**Doe**	Finance	Auditor	454

6   Why do people and organisations use databases? Discuss with the group.

Example: They use databases to find out … .

Data processing

1 Match the headings in the box to the data processing steps a–f.

> data coding   data collection   data entry   data sorting
> data tabulation   data validation

a _____ Gather the raw data which you want to process. `1`

b _____ Arrange and systemise the data.

c _____ Clean the data and double-check for faults and inconsistencies.

d _____ Enter the data into a system.

e _____ Arrange the data into table format so that it can be analysed.

f _____ Create categories to organise the data into relevant groups.

2 Put the data processing steps in 1 into the correct order.

3 ▶ 🔊 **25** Listen to an IT expert describing the data processing steps to a colleague. Check your answers to 1 and 2.

4 ▶ 🔊 **26** Listen and mark the syllable stress in these nouns and verbs.

1 entry
2 collection
3 tabulation
4 validation
5 sorting
6 coding
7 gather
8 create
9 arrange
10 enter
11 double-check
12 format

5 Listen again and repeat the words.

Vocabulary **6** Complete these sentences with the words in the box.

about	at	between	for	from	in	into	of	~~to~~

Example: This database is used <u>to</u> store our financial information.

1 What's the difference _____ a database and a spreadsheet?
2 A database is _____ storing data.
3 The school has information _____ students.
4 Can people access the system _____ the same time?
5 A database is a collection _____ records.
6 You retrieve information _____ the database.
7 You enter the data _____ the system.
8 Which software do you use _____ your work?

Language

Quick questions to check understanding	
We use these when we are making sure the other person understands the statement.	*That's called collection.* **OK**?
	That's coding? **Got that**?
	That's tabulation. **All right**?
	We call that sorting. **Understood**?

Speaking **7** Work in pairs. Explain the data processing steps from 1 in your own words.

8 Look at the examples of database software below. What database software do you know? What is it used for?

Data storage and backup

Vocabulary **1** Match the data storage and backup solutions in the box to pictures A–F. What other solutions are there?

| external hard drive | hard disk | mp3 player | server | the Internet |
| usb flash drive | | | | |

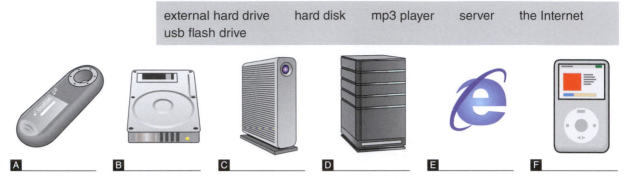

A _____ B _____ C _____ D _____ E _____ F _____

Reading **2** Read this article about data storage. Complete the sentences with the words in the box.

| cloud | contents | emerging | encrypt | flash | loss | magnetic |
| ~~offsite~~ | protect | security | theft | volumes | |

Data storage

Online storage is an (1) _offsite_ method of data storage and back-up. A remote server with a network connection and special software backs up files, folders, or the entire (2) _____ of a hard drive. There are many companies that provide a web-based backup.

One (3) _____ technology in this area is (4) _____ computing. This allows colleagues in an organisation to share resources, software and information over the Internet.

Continuous backup and storage on a remote hard drive eliminates the risk of data (5) _____ as a result of fire, flood or (6) _____ . Remote data storage and back-up providers (7) _____ the data and set up password protection to ensure maximum (8) _____ .

Small businesses and individuals choose to save data in a more traditional way. External drives, disks and (9) _____ tapes are very popular data storage solutions. USB or (10) _____ memories, DVDs and hard disks are cheap and widely accessible solutions. These methods are very practical with small (11) _____ of data storage and backup. However, they are not very reliable and do not (12) _____ the user in case of a disaster.

Salesforce
Microsoft
Google
Yahoo
Amazon
Zoho
Rackspace

Speaking **3** What storage and backup solutions are the most popular? Which solutions do you use most often?

Listening **4** 🔊 27 Listen and repeat these phrases.

1 emerging technology
2 cloud computing
3 data storage
4 hard drive
5 external drives
6 backup providers

5 🔊 28 Listen to this dialogue. A colleague, Tim, is asking an IT expert, Sandy, what storage device to buy. Mark these statements true (T) or false (F).

1	Tim needs the storage device for work.	T / F
2	Tim wants to backup music and photos.	T / F
3	Sandy recommends an external hard drive.	T / F
4	Tim can spend $300 on the storage device.	T / F
5	Sandy recommends a storage device with a special feature.	T / F

Language

Asking for and giving advice

	I/You/He/She/It/We/They **should/shouldn't (should not)** … .
We use **should/would** + infinitive without *to* to give advice.	*What* **should** *I* **do**? *You* **should buy** *a flash drive.* *You* **shouldn't get** *a server.*
	I/You/He/She/It/We/They **would/wouldn't (would not)** … .
	What **would** *you* **recommend**? *I'd* **(would) recommend** *a flash drive.* *I* **wouldn't (would not) recommend** *a server.*

Speaking **6** Work in pairs. Practise asking for advice about backup solutions for a small company. Use the information in 2.

Example:
A: *What would you recommend … ?*
B: *I'd recommend … . /You should … .*

Database system benefits

Speaking   **1**   What kind of data do companies create, manipulate, store and retrieve?

Vocabulary   **2**   Match the company department 1–8 with the type of data it works with a– h.

1	Finance	a) data about employees, training, recruitment needs
2	Marketing	b) data about product specification, details and design
3	Human resources	c) data about profits, tax, loans, shares and cash
4	Customer relations	d) data about volume of products sold
5	Production	e) data about customers, satisfaction surveys, promotions
6	Technical support	f) data about product advertisements and competitors
7	Sales	g) data about quantity of product in storage
8	Stock management	h) information about the Help Desk, support calls, manuals, problem reports

3   Look at the four types of data below from PartyPlanner Ltd. What do you think PartyPlanner Ltd does? What company departments can you identify?

Personal data:
- CVs, job descriptions
- employee personal data
- training
- holiday

Customer data:
- customer contacts
- satisfaction surveys
- promotions

Product data:
- inventory
- purchasing needs
- return products

Technical data:
- contact to help desk
- helpdesk reports
- troubleshooting manuals
- service reports

Speaking   **4**   Work in small groups. Talk about the advantages and disadvantages of a computerised database. Present your ideas to the rest of the group.

Example: There are many advantages/disadvantages … .

Business matters

Reading **1** Read part of this email from the owner of Jumbo Book Store. Answer these questions.

1 What types of information does Jumbo Book Store communicate between its employees?
2 How do the employees exchange information in the company?
3 What documents does Amiki prepare?
4 How much time does it take to compile the data?
5 Why do the customers complain?

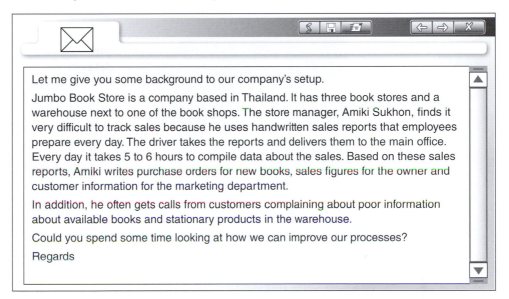

Let me give you some background to our company's setup.

Jumbo Book Store is a company based in Thailand. It has three book stores and a warehouse next to one of the book shops. The store manager, Amiki Sukhon, finds it very difficult to track sales because he uses handwritten sales reports that employees prepare every day. The driver takes the reports and delivers them to the main office. Every day it takes 5 to 6 hours to compile data about the sales. Based on these sales reports, Amiki writes purchase orders for new books, sales figures for the owner and customer information for the marketing department.

In addition, he often gets calls from customers complaining about poor information about available books and stationary products in the warehouse.

Could you spend some time looking at how we can improve our processes?

Regards

Speaking **2** Work in small groups. Prepare recommendations using the problem/solution outline.

Problem/Solution Outline

Problem	Who? What? Why?

Solutions	1. 2.	3. 4.

End Results	

3 Present your recommendations to another group.

5

E-commerce

- talk about e-commerce companies and websites
- talk about quantity
- talk about future arrangements
- present a plan

E-commerce companies

Speaking **1** What products or services do you usually buy online? What products do you not buy online? Why?

Listening **2** 🔊 29 Listen to this interview with David Aston. He works for a company that sells home cleaning products. Mark the statements true (T) or false (F).

1 David's company sells mainly online.   T / F
2 70% of their business is online.   T / F
3 People buy their cleaning products when they buy their food.   T / F
4 People buy their cleaning products in supermarkets.   T / F
5 Online sales are growing.   T / F

Language

Talking about quantity

We use **many** and **a few** with countable plural nouns.	We need **a few** users to test this. They don't have **many** customers.
We use **much** and **a little** with uncountable nouns.	We have **a little** money for online shopping each week. I don't have **much** knowledge on that subject.
We use **a lot of** and **some** with countable and uncountable nouns.	**A lot of** businesses need E-commerce upgrades. **Some** money has been kept aside for this.

3 Choose the correct words to complete these sentences.

1 *A lot of/Much* shops have online presence. They sell *many/much* products online.
2 *Some/A little* companies offer customer service and advice on their E-commerce websites.
3 I don't have *much/many* knowledge of computers, but I can still shop online.
4 Companies spend *a lot of/many* money on E-commerce security.
5 Even when companies only have *a little/a few* money for online marketing, they should spend it.

Listening **4** [CD 30] Listen and repeat these phrases.
1 not a lot of time
2 too much work
3 only a little money
4 a few computers
5 a lot of memory

Speaking **5** Work in pairs. Use the words in the Language box on page 36 to talk about your own online shopping habits.

*Example: I buy **a lot of** music online but I get **few** clothes online.*

Vocabulary **6** Match the types of business in the box to the correct column 1–4.

> B2C business-to-consumer   C2C consumer-to-consumer
> B2B business-to-business   M-commerce

Types of Business	1 _____	2 _____	3 _____	4 _____
Explanation	Companies exchange information and make wholesale transactions.	Companies sell products or services to customers over the Internet.	People sell or exchange second-hand, used items and collectibles.	Customers purchase products and services via mobile devices.
Examples	coffee supplier to Nestlé	Amazon	eBay	news, sport results

7 Give examples of the four types of business in 6.

Writing **8** What are the advantages and disadvantages of shopping online? Use this table to make notes and then make sentences.

Example: There's more choice online but you can see things better in a shop.

	advantages	disadvantages
security		
speed		
choice		
convenience		
price		

Speaking **9** Present your ideas to the group.

E-commerce features

Speaking **1** Work in small groups. What are the features of this website?

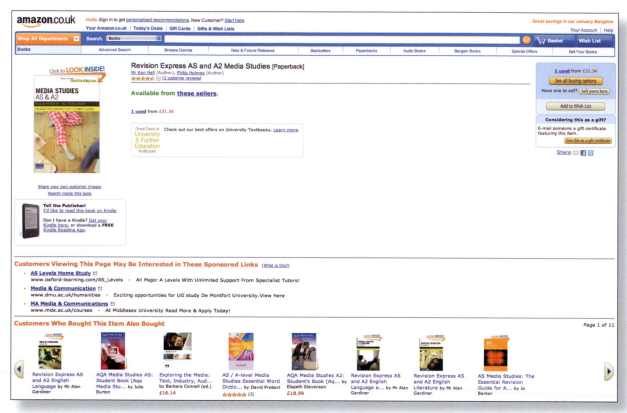

Vocabulary **2** What are the steps in buying products online? Number these sentences in the correct order.

a) The customer opens an account.

b) The customer goes to the check-out.

c) The customer puts the item(s) in a basket or shopping cart.

d) The customer pays for the product(s) with a credit or debit card.

e) The customer goes to the website. `1`

f) The customer searches and/or browses the website.

g) The customer chooses the item(s) to buy.

h) The customers checks the order.

Listening **3** 🔊 **31** Listen and repeat these phrases.

1 open an account

2 go to the checkout

3 put an item in the basket

4 browse the website

5 choose an item

6 check the order

Speaking **4** Work in pairs. Use *firstly, secondly, then, after that, finally* to describe the steps in buying a product or service. Talk about something you have bought, like a DVD or an airline ticket.

Language

Reading **5** Complete this text with the words in the box.

and	but	or	so

> Companies want to reach more customers, (1) _____ they go online. It is easy to set up an online business (2) _____ it is difficult to design and develop a website that attracts a lot of customers. Hardware (3) _____ software provide basic infrastructure for E-commerce.
>
> Networking, customer interface and payment solutions are very important parts of a company's E-commerce solution. Customers expect a fast and reliable service (4) _____ they will go somewhere else to buy things.

Vocabulary **6** Match the first half of the sentences 1–6 to to the second half a–f.

1 Effective product information and
2 Customers can use their credit cards, PayPal or
3 We used a lot of promotions, so
4 I don't know how to buy online but
5 They want to buy a Cat 5e cable so
6 In E-commerce you can look at a picture of a product but

a) I'll check online tutorials.
b) electronic cheques to pay for transactions.
c) you can't touch it.
d) our sales improved a lot.
e) they search the Internet.
f) promotions attract customers.

Speaking **7** Work in small groups. Talk about an E-commerce website you know and like. Say what is good about it. Use *and, so, but* and *or*.

Example: I like the B&Q website. It has … and … .

Transaction security

Speaking **1** What are the potential security threats to online shopping? Share your ideas with the group.

Reading **2** Read this email. Answer these questions.

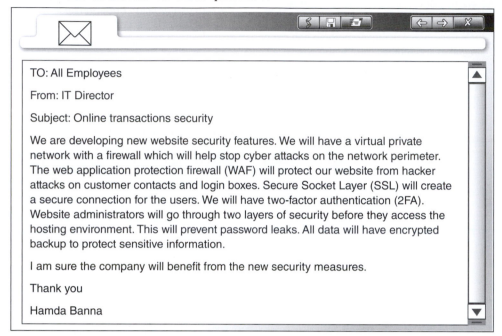

TO: All Employees

From: IT Director

Subject: Online transactions security

We are developing new website security features. We will have a virtual private network with a firewall which will help stop cyber attacks on the network perimeter. The web application protection firewall (WAF) will protect our website from hacker attacks on customer contacts and login boxes. Secure Socket Layer (SSL) will create a secure connection for the users. We will have two-factor authentication (2FA). Website administrators will go through two layers of security before they access the hosting environment. This will prevent password leaks. All data will have encrypted backup to protect sensitive information.

I am sure the company will benefit from the new security measures.

Thank you

Hamda Banna

1 How many security features will the company have?
2 Which security feature will stop attacks on the company network?
3 What solution will protect customer contacts and login boxes?
4 What will protect private user information sent over the network?
5 What will the two-factor authentication prevent?
6 What will protect information?

Language

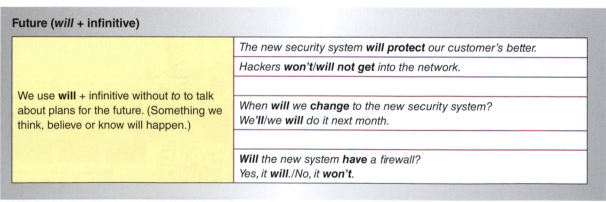

Future (*will* + infinitive)

We use **will** + infinitive without *to* to talk about plans for the future. (Something we think, believe or know will happen.)	*The new security system **will protect** our customer's better.*
	*Hackers **won't**/**will not get** into the network.*
	*When **will** we **change** to the new security system? We'll/we **will** do it next month.*
	***Will** the new system **have** a firewall? Yes, it **will**./No, it **won't**.*

Listening **3** 🔊 32 Listen and repeat these sentences.

1 The company won't provide Internet access to all employees.
2 I'll do the security checks and then upgrade this week.
3 When will you finish the work?
4 Yes, I will.
5 No, she won't.

Speaking **4** Work in small groups. Talk about your organisation's plans or your own plans for the future. Ask and answer each other questions.

Example:
A: We'll open a new office in Singapore.
B: When will you open it?
A: Next year.

Vocabulary **5** Match the labels in the network diagram A–H with the items 1–8.

1 the Internet
2 the local area network
3 the hardware firewall (with a router)
4 computers with firewall software
5 outbound traffic
6 inbound traffic
7 restricted traffic
8 allowed traffic

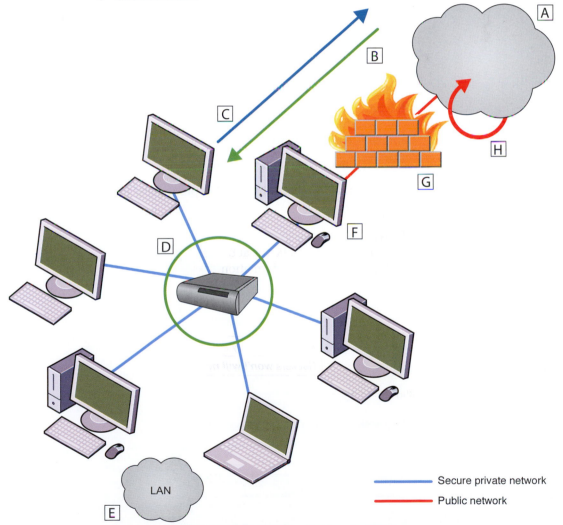

Speaking **6** You are setting up a new computer workstation with a network connection. Your client wants to use the set-up for online purchases, bank dealing and financial transactions securely. Talk about what security solution you will install. Present your solution to the group.

Online transactions

1 Shayan is telling Monika how customers will pay for something online on a new website. Complete this dialogue with the words in the box.

accounts	bank	completes	confirmation	customer	First
gateway	payment	rejection	web		

Monika: Shayan, can you explain how a customer (1) _____ an online transaction?

Shayan: OK, it's very easy. (2) _____ the customer will place an order. The seller's (3) _____ server will confirm availability of the product and send a response. After that, the customer checks out and completes the (4) _____ instructions. Then the server will send a payment request to a payment (5) _____ . The payment gateway will check the buyer's ability to pay with the (6) _____ . OK?

Monika: Fine. Go on.

Shayan: The bank will respond and send payment acceptance or (7) _____ to the seller's web server through the payment gateway. Finally, the customer will receive the server response with the order (8) _____ or rejection.

Monika: Will the (9) _____ have to register?

Shayan: Yes, all buyers must have their (10) _____ before they complete the transaction.

Monika: Thank you. Now I understand.

Listening **2** ▶ 33 Listen and check your answers.

Speaking **3** Complete the flowchart of the online purchasing process. Then explain it to your partner.

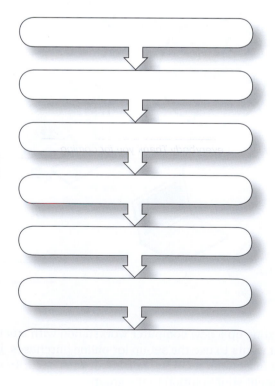

Business matters

Writing **1** You work for SellOnline.com. The company develops E-commerce solutions for small businesses. Your client, Document Ltd, sells stationery. They sell lots of different types of product. Document Ltd wants to develop its online presence to reach customers more effectively. Complete the proposal template. Use these questions to help you.

1 What type of E-commerce will Document Ltd offer?
2 What E-commerce technologies will Document Ltd use to attract customers?
3 What security solutions will the company set up in order to protect both the customer and the company?
4 What tools and features will the company website have?
5 How will the customer complete transactions?

Proposal No. 2011/123/45	**Date:**
Customer:	**Business activity:**
Subject:	
E-commerce type:	
E-commerce technologies:	
Security solutions:	
Website features and tools:	
Transaction process:	
Proposal presented by:	

Language

Useful phrases for presentations	
Introduction	Good morning/afternoon everybody. Thank you for coming.
	Today we are going to present … .
	First, I am going to talk about … .
	Then, we will show you … .
	Finally, we will answer your questions … .
Speakers	Now, I'll hand over to my colleague.
	Let me start with … .
Closing	To finish … .
	Thank you very much for listening. Are there any questions?

Speaking **2** Prepare and deliver a presentation for the marketing director of Document Ltd. Use your proposal from 1 to help you.

6

Network systems

- describe networks
- make recommendations and suggestions
- talk about the past
- talk about network range and speeds

Types of network

Speaking   **1**   What computer networks do you use in your work or studies? What do you use the networks for? How do you access the networks?

Listening   **2**   ▶ 🌐 34   Agatha is the owner of a small flower shop. Katharina is a network architect. Agatha needs some advice from Katharina about a network solution for her company. Listen and answer these questions.

1. What does Agatha think she should do?
2. What does Katharina recommend?
3. What does Katharina say she will do?
4. When does Agatha want the network to be ready?

Reading   **3**   Read Katharina's email to Agatha. Complete this email with the words in the box.

equipment	Internet	LAN	recommend
remote	should	VPN	WAN

✉

📎 💾 🗐   ⬅ ➡ ✕

Dear Agatha

Following our meeting last week, please find my recommendations for your business.

I think you (1) _____ set up a LAN, or Local Area Network, and a WAN, or Wide Area Network, for your needs. A (2) _____ connects devices over a small area, for example your apartment and the shop. In addition, you should connect office (3) _____ , such as the printer, scanner and fax machine, to your LAN because you can then share these devices between users.

I'd recommend that we connect the LAN to a (4) _____ so you can link to the Internet and sell your products. In addition, I'd (5) _____ we set up a Virtual Private Network so that you have a (6) _____ access to your company's LAN, when you travel.

(7) _____ is a private network that uses a public network, usually the (8) _____ , to connect remote sites or users together.

Let's meet on Friday to discuss these recommendations.

Best regards

Katharina

Language

Speaking **4** Look at the three network solutions. What are the differences?

5 Which network solution would you recommend for a large corporation or organisation, a small business and a family home? Why?

I'd recommend solution 1 for … because … .

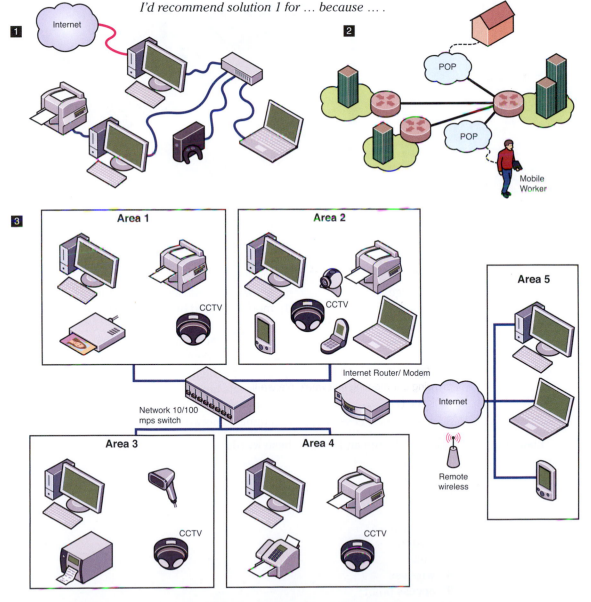

Writing **6** Write a description of the network solution you use at work or at home. Which of the the three solutions in 4 is it most like? Why?

Networking hardware

Speaking **1** Which of the items below do you know? What are they? What do they do?

2 Work in pairs. Make a list of all the networking hardware you can think of. Compare your list with another pair.

Vocabulary **3** Match the words 1–8 to the descriptions a–g.

1	a modem	a) is an entrance to another network
2	a repeater	b) channels incoming data but maintains the bandwidth speed
3	a bridge	c) allows wireless devices to connect to the network
4	a router	d) modulates and demodulates the data into a digital or an analog signal
5	a gateway	e) channels incoming data but shares the bandwidth among the devices present on a network
6	a switch	f) sends the digital signal further on in the network
7	a hub	g) connects networks and sends packages of data between them
8	a wireless access point	h) connects networks that use the same protocol

Listening **4** ▶ 🔊 35 Listen and repeat these words.

1 modem
2 repeater
3 bridge
4 router
5 gateway
6 switch
7 hub
8 wireless
9 access point
10 network connectors
11 network interface card

Reading **5** Complete this dialogue with the words in the box.

about	change	devices	necessary	problem
speed	should	user	What	

Boris: I have a problem with the network download (1) _____ . What can you suggest?

Ahsan: Why don't you (2) _____ the hub?

Boris: I don't think that will work. The hub is fine.

Ahsan: OK. How (3) _____ adding a repeater then?

Boris: Hmm, I'm not sure it will help. It's not a (4) _____ with the signal strength.

Ahsan: OK, then you should check the cables and network (5) _____ to make sure that they are compatible with your network.

Boris: (6) _____ about changing the modem?

Ahsan: I don't think it's (7) _____ . I think it's a problem with the bridge, switch or the router. You (8) _____ look at the specifications.

Boris: OK, I will. Thanks for your help.

Ahsan: Why don't you check (9) _____ recommendations on the Internet as well?

Boris: Good idea. I'll do that.

Listening **6** [▶ 36] Listen and check your answers.

Language

Making suggestions
We can make suggestions with:

Why don't we/you + infinitive without *to*.	**Why don't you call** the IT help desk? *That's a good idea.*
What about + *-ing*	**What about buying** a new router? *I don't think that will work.*
How about + *-ing*	**How about reading** the instructions first? *I'll do that.*

Listening **7** [▶ 37] Listen and repeat these suggestions.

1 Why don't you change the modem?
2 How about connecting a repeater?
3 What about looking on the website?

Vocabulary **8** Complete these sentences with the words in the box.

between	on	over	to	with

1 Is this software compatible _____ this computer?
2 A LAN connects devices _____ a small area.
3 Is the computer connected _____ the modem?
4 The LAN allows you to share information _____ users.
5 Why don't you look _____ the Internet?

Speaking **9** What problems do you have with networks? Work in pairs. Make a list. Think about speed, compatibility, hardware and software.

10 Show your list to another pair. Ask for help and suggest solutions.

Example:
A: *This software doesn't work with this … .*
B: *Why don't you … ?*

Talking about the past

Reading **1** How much do you know about the history of networking? Can you match these events 1–4 to the dates a–d?

1 The creation of the World Wide Web
2 The start of Facebook
3 The launch of Twitter
4 The beginning of MySpace

a) 2006
b) 1990
c) 2003
d) 2004

Speaking **2** What social networks do you use? How much time do you spend on them?

Example: I use … . I spend about … .

Reading **3** Read this text about Karl's IT career up until now and answer these questions.

> 'I left school in Cambridge in the UK at the age of 18 and went straight to the University of Bristol to study computing in 2000. I graduated in 2004 and decided to travel around the world for a year.
>
> In 2006 I got a job back in Cambridge with the software company Arm. I stayed with Arm for two years and then went to work for Microsoft in Seattle in the USA. This is where I am now and I love it!'

1 When did Karl go to university?
2 When did he leave university?
3 What did he do after university?
4 Where did Karl go in 2006?
5 When did he go to Seattle?

Language

Past simple (1)

We use the **past simple** tense to talk about finished actions in the past.	*When did I/she/he/we/they create the network?* *She **created** the network in December 2008.* *I **started** the network last year.*
Time expressions	*I looked at that **yesterday**.* *I had broadband connected **three days/a month/two years ago**.* *I used that system **last week/year/month**.* *I started that user group **on Monday/in June/in 2001**.*

Listening 4   ▶ 💿 38   Listen and repeat these sentences.

1 When did they start work?
2 They installed the computers yesterday.
3 We didn't work last week.
4 She went to the office on Sunday.
5 Did you finish the report?

Speaking 5 Practise asking and answering questions about what you did yesterday or last week in your work or studies.

Example:
A: *What did you do last week?*
B: *I worked on the new network.*

6 Talk about what you did on your last day off.

Example:
A: *What did you do on your day off?*
B: *I went to the gym.*

Language

Past simple (2)

Regular past tense endings	*look*	***looked***
	use	***used***
	install	***installed***
	connect	***connected***
	work	***worked***
Irregular past tense endings	*set up*	***set up***
	go	***went***
	see	***saw***
	do	***did***
	buy	***bought***
	be	***was***

Writing 7 Write three or four sentences about your own computing education and/or work up until now. Use the text in 3 to help you.

Speaking 8 Work in pairs. Ask and answer questions about your education and/or work.

Network range and speed

Listening **1**   ▶ 💿 **39**   Listen and complete this dialogue between Karoline and Sam.

Karoline: How do you describe network speed?

Sam: In bits, kilobits, megabits and gigabits. They describe network speed. For example, dial-up connections allow (1) _____ kilobits per second and DSL from (2) _____ kilobits per second to (3) _____ megabits per second.

Karoline: OK. I've got that. What about the range?

Sam: Range is the distance of network coverage, so distance units represent network range. Most countries use metric but some use feet as units of measurement. Metres or feet usually describe the range of a network. Home networking routers support a range up to (4) _____ feet or (5) _____ metres indoors and (6) _____ feet or (7) _____ metres outdoors.

Karoline: Thanks.

2   ▶ 💿 **40**   Listen and repeat these speeds and ranges.

1. 77 kilobits per second
2. 5 megabits a second
3. 2 gigabits per minute
4. 250 metres
5. 40 feet

Speaking **3**   Say these speeds and ranges.

1	156 feet	4	7,000 metres
2	12 kbit/s	5	95 Mbit/s
3	4 Gbit/m	6	65 Mbit/s

4   Write down four speeds and ranges and dictate them to your partner.

Reading **5**   Read these texts and answer these questions.

> ### Range
>
> Wireless networks have limited range. Network range depends on the type of 802.11 protocol, strength of the device transmitter and the architecture of the surrounding area. Some structures, such as walls and metal frames, reduce the range of a WLAN by 25%. However, users can extend the range of a WLAN. Repeaters forward the wireless signal to access points or routers and increase the range of a network.
>
> ### Speed
>
> Bandwidth and latency are the measures of computer network speed, or data transfer rate. Bandwidth is the maximum throughput of data in bits per second.
>
> Some modems support 100 Gbit/s but speed depends on the hardware and software used. Latency is the delay that network creates during the transfer data. Users have no, or very little, control over bandwidth and latency.

1. How many things does network range depend on?
2. What can reduce network range?
3. What can improve network range?
4. What two things affect speed?

Business matters

Reading **1** Karam and Natasha work for the ComHelp company. The company provides IT services to customers. Karam and Natasha work in different areas of the city. Every week they write a report for their boss. Read their notes.

	Monday	Tuesday	Wednesday	Thursday	Friday
Natasha	called CISCO about a training do paperwork	went to British Council to install new software	attended the training on network cabling	day off	had a meeting with the team
Karam	went to TESCO to fix Cat6 cables	set up LAN in a paper factory	day off	installed an audio/video server in Welcare hospital	
You					

Writing **2** Complete the table in 1 with notes about what you did last week at work or college.

3 Write a report about what you did last week.
Example: Last week I … . On Monday I … and … .

Speaking **4** Roleplay the following situation. Explain to your boss why you were not in the office.
Student A: Turn to page 68
Student B: Turn to page 78

IT support

- talk about results of an action
- write service reports
- explain the use of things
- deal with problems

Fault diagnosis

Speaking **1** Work in pairs. Make a list of computer hardware problems. Compare your list with another pair.

Reading **2** Read this dialogue and complete it with the words in the box.

checked	disconnected	found	go	switched	type	tight
unplugged	worked	working				

Haider: Hello, IT Help Desk.
Maryam: Hi, this is Maryam from Human Resources.
Haider: Hi, this is Haider. How can I help you, Maryam?
Maryam: I (1) _____ my computer off yesterday and today I can't turn it on.
Haider: What (2) _____ of computer do you have?
Maryam: I'm not sure. It's a desktop computer. It (3) _____ fine yesterday.
Haider: Don't worry. Have you (4) _____ the cable connections?
Maryam: No, I haven't. I can see some cables but I don't know which cable goes where.
Haider: Make sure all cables are (5) _____ and fully plugged in.
Maryam: Ok, give me a sec. Oh, I think I've (6) _____ the problem. I have one cable that is (7) _____ . It's the power cable. Where does it go?
Haider: The power cable should (8) _____ in the three-pronged port on the computer.
Maryam: OK, done. Let me try now. It's (9) _____ fine. Sorry about that. Stupid of me.
Haider: Maybe the cleaners (10) _____ your PC by mistake last night.
Maryam: Maybe. Good, we've solved the problem. Thank you, Haider.
Haider: You're welcome. Have a good day.
Maryam: You too.

Listening **3** ▶ 🎵 41 Listen and check your answers.

4 ▶ 🔊 **42** Listen and repeat these words.

1	checked	3	unplugged	5	disconnected
2	switched	4	worked		

Language

Present perfect

We use the **present perfect** tense to talk about recent actions (an action that has happened in the past and has a result in the present).	*I've unplugged the computer.*
	She hasn't finished the report.
	Has she switched off the computer? *Yes, she has./No, she hasn't.*
	Have you checked the cable connections? *Yes, I have. /No, I haven't.*

We use **have/has** + the past participle of the verb. (To form the past participle of **regular** verbs, we add *-ed*.)	*clean*	**cleaned**
	work	**worked**
Irregular past participles	*do*	**done**
	be	**been**
	run	**run**
	see	**seen**
	have	**had**
	make	**made**

5 Complete these questions with *have* or *has* and the correct form of the verb in brackets.

1 _____ you _____ (run) the computer in the battery mode?
2 How long _____ you _____ (have) the iPad?
3 _____ you _____ (charge) the battery?
4 _____ he _____ (open) the file?
5 _____ she _____ (enter) her username and password?
6 _____ they _____ (change) the Internet Service Provider?
7 _____ you _____ (check) the remaining disk space?
8 _____ you _____ (install) or _____ (uninstall) software recently?
9 _____ Dillip _____ (update) the drivers recently?

6 Use the present perfect to make positive or negative sentences.

Example: the screen/go/blank
The screen's gone blank.
1 the charger/stop/working
2 I/not upgrade/the operating system
3 She/not/install/the updates
4 They/reinstall/the application
5 She/not/be able to fix the problem
6 I/defragment/your drive

Listening 7 ▶ 🔊 **43** Listen and repeat the questions in 5.

Speaking 8 Work in pairs. Practise a phone call to the company IT help desk.

Student A: Turn to page 69.
Student B: Turn to page 79.

Software repair

1 🖮 **44** You work for SoftwareHelp.com as a helpdesk technician. Listen to three phone calls and complete the second and third tickets.

1

Help Desk ticket	
Date	5.05
Name	Bolek
Problem	Word file won't open in Office.
Contact	0504445553
Service Person	Alex

2

Help Desk ticket	
Date	
Name	
Problem	
Contact	
Service Person	

3

Help Desk ticket	
Date	
Name	
Problem	
Contact	
Service Person	

2 Work in pairs. Compare your notes in the three tickets. Is your information the same? Listen again and check.

Speaking **3** What other software problems do computer users often have? Discuss with the group.

Example: Computer users often ... .

Reading **4** Complete the service reports for the IT support team. Use the information in the three tickets and the words in the box.

| Check | file | install | move | resend | run |
| saved | version | version | viruses | | |

1

Service Report	
Date	6.05
Name	Bolek
Fault diagnosis questions	1 What (1) _____ of Office do you have? 2 What is the version of the (2) _____ ?
Possible solutions	1 If you have newer version, (3) _____ an Office patch. 2 Ask the sender to save the file in an older version and (4) _____ it.

2

Service Report	
Date	17.06
Name	Sara
Fault diagnosis questions	1 Have you (5) _____ the file? 2 Are there any messages about (6) _____ in the attachment?
Possible solutions	1 (7) _____ the attachment changes. 2 Look for the file in Internet Temporary Files.

3

Service Report	
Date	14.07
Name	Sylvia
Fault diagnosis questions	1 What (8) _____ of Office do you have? 2 Have you checked the Recycle Bin? 3 Have you (9) _____ disk defragmenter recently?
Possible solutions	1 If the file is in the Recycle Bin, (10) _____ it to a folder in My Documents. 2 If the file isn't in the Recycle Bin, install undeleted software.

Speaking **5** Work in pairs. Practise three phone conversations between the IT support team and Bolek, Sara and Sylvia. Use the information in the three tickets in 1 and the service reports.

Example:
A: Good morning. How can I help you?
B: My name is Bolek and I have a problem with opening a file.

Hardware repair

Reading   **1**   Label the diagram with these tools (in bold) from the advertisement.

This kit has all the tools you'll require to fix a computer.

- There is a **reversible ratchet driver** with 20 different sized bits, a 6-inch flathead **screwdriver**, a reversible 1/8-inch mini screwdriver, a **hex key set** and 5-inch, long nose **pliers**.

- This set also has a 5-inch **wire-cutter/stripper**, an I.C. **insertion/extraction clipper**, a **three prong holder**, **tweezers**, a spare parts box with parts, an **anti-static wrist strap**, and a black zipper case.

The tools are demagnetized so your system and magnetic media is safe from any damage.

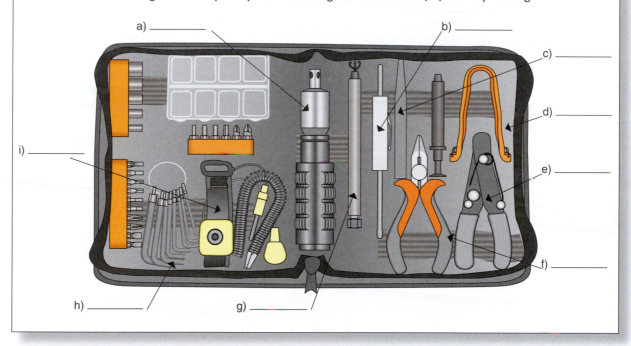

a) _____   b) _____   c) _____   d) _____   e) _____   f) _____   g) _____   h) _____   i) _____

Listening   **2**   🔊 45   Listen and repeat the names of the tools in the kit.

Vocabulary   **3**   Match the tool 1–8 to its use a–h.

1. reversible ratchet driver
2. screwdriver
3. hex key
4. pliers
5. wire cutter/stripper
6. insertion/extraction clipper
7. tweezers
8. anti-static wrist strap

a) used for inserting and removing fibre connectors in tight spaces
b) used to prevent electrostatic discharge
c) used for tightening and removing screws
d) used for easy driving of screws and nuts
e) used to hold small objects
f) used to hold objects, cut or bend tough materials
g) used to drive bolts and screws into a hexagonal socket
h) used for cutting wire or removing the insulation

Language

Speaking **4** Work in pairs. Talk about the tools you use with computers. Say what you use them for.

Reading **5** Match the diagnostic tools 1–4 to the descriptions a–d.

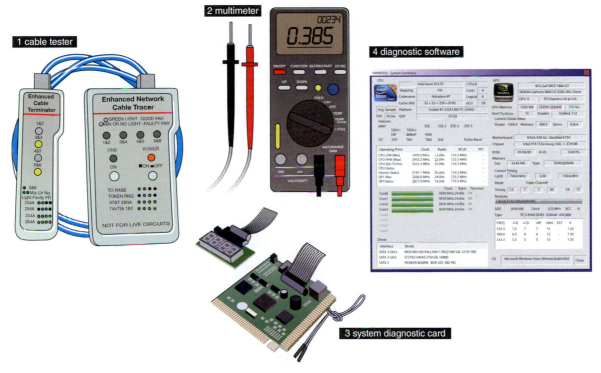

a) It measures electrical properties such as AC or DC voltage, current and resistance. It troubleshoots electrical problems in batteries, power supplies, and wiring systems.

b) It is an electronic device that checks the electrical connections in wired devices.

c) It checks the system and identifies problems in different areas of the computer hardware. It usually checks the computer's memory, keyboard, monitor, system processor and hard disk speed.

d) It is a device which tests the operation of the system as it boots up. It identifies system errors when the system is dead or unable to start from the hard disk or CD.

6 Now answer these questions.

1 What is a multimeter used for?
2 What is the cable tester used for?
3 What is a system diagnostic card used for?
4 What is the diagnostic software used for?

Customer service

Speaking **1** Look at the cartoon. How do people react when there is a problem with their computer? Why?

Listening **2** ▶ 🖭 **46** Listen to a phone call to a company IT help desk. Choose the correct answers a, b or c, to the questions.

1 What is Tuka's problem?
a) can't print out   b) has lost files   c) is not connected to the network
2 How does Tuka sound?
a) worried   b) angry   c) tired
3 What is the possible cause of the problem?
a) a hardware upgrade   b) a server problem   c) a software upgrade
4 What is the help desk technician's first suggestion?
a) go to a folder on the server   b) go to a folder on the desktop
c) go to a folder on the C drive
5 What is the help desk technician's second suggestion?
a) He will call back in five minutes.   b) He will come down to Tuka's office.
c) He will get help from someone else.

3 Listen again and complete the technician's sentences.

1 How can I _____ you?
2 I _____ .
3 I'm _____ we can find your file.
4 _____ go to the search box ... .
5 Good _____ .

4 ▶ 🖭 **47** Listen and repeat the technician's sentences.

Writing **5** Work in pairs. Write a short dialogue between an IT help desk technician and a colleague about a software or hardware problem. Use the phrases from 3.

Speaking **6** Work in pairs. Read your dialogues to the rest of the class.

Business matters

Reading **1** You work as an IT help desk technician. You are responsible for these tickets from colleagues in your company. Read the tickets. What are the problems?

Help Desk ticket	
Date	10.11
Name	Ben
Problem	I can't print out.
Contact	0504446231
Service Person	You

Help Desk ticket	
Date	11.11
Name	Clare
Problem	I can't connect to the network.
Contact	0504445558
Service Person	You

Help Desk ticket	
Date	12.11
Name	Simone
Problem	My computer fan is very noisy.
Contact	0504446553
Service Person	You

Writing **2** Choose one of the Help Desk tickets from 1. Write questions for the fault diagnosis and possible solutions.

Example: Is there an error message on your screen? What does it say?
Have you tried restarting your computer?

Service Report	
Date	
Name	
Fault diagnosis questions	
Possible solutions	

Speaking **3** Work in pairs. Roleplay the conversations about the problems. Student A is the help desk technician and Student B is the colleague.

8

IT security and safety

- talk about security solutions
- express possibility and prohibition
- report events and incidents
- recommend improvement actions

Security solutions

Speaking **1** Work in pairs. Make a list of all the different words about security threats and attacks you can think of.

Reading **2** Read the descriptions 1–8. Match the words in the box to the descriptions.

| adware | hacker | browser hijacker | malware attack | spyware |
| Trojan | virus | worm | | |

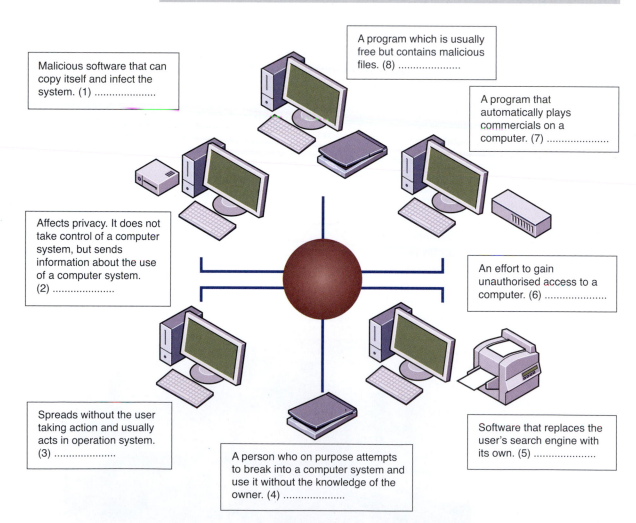

A program which is usually free but contains malicious files. (8) ....

Malicious software that can copy itself and infect the system. (1) ....

A program that automatically plays commercials on a computer. (7) ....

Affects privacy. It does not take control of a computer system, but sends information about the use of a computer system. (2) ....

An effort to gain unauthorised access to a computer. (6) ....

Spreads without the user taking action and usually acts in operation system. (3) ....

A person who on purpose attempts to break into a computer system and use it without the knowledge of the owner. (4) ....

Software that replaces the user's search engine with its own. (5) ....

Speaking **3** Have you ever had a computer security threat? Has anyone ever hacked into your computer system? Use the words and phrases in 2 to describe what happened.

4 Work in small groups. Discuss what you can do to stop these problems.

Vocabulary **5** Match the security solution 1–5 to its purpose a–e.

1 a firewall
2 antivirus software

3 authentication
4 username, password and biometric scanning
5 encryption

a) prevents damage that viruses might cause
b) make sure only authorised people access the network
c) checks the user is allowed to use system
d) blocks unauthorised access codes
e) protects the system from public access

Listening **6** ▶ 🖫 48 Listen to this dialogue and answer the questions. Ludek has asked his IT expert friend, Ales, for help.

1 Why does Ludek want Ales to check his laptop?
2 Why is Ludek worried that he may lose his project?
3 What does Ales think has happened to Ludek's laptop?
4 Why does he recommend Ludek installs an anti-spyware software?
5 Why is it important to have a network access password?
6 What will Ales do for Ludek?

Language

Expressing possibility	
We use **may/might** + infinitive without *to* to talk about things that are possible now or in the future.	*You **may** have a virus on your computer.*
	*The program **might** not run properly.*

Speaking **7** Work in pairs. Practise giving advice to a non-IT expert on protecting their computer.

Example:
Non-IT expert: What should I do to stop … ?
Expert: You should … . It may/might … .

Workstation health and safety

Speaking   **1**   Work in pairs. Make a list of computer health and safety problems. Compare your list with another pair.

Vocabulary   **2**   Label this diagram with the advice 1–8.

     1   There should be clearance under the work surface.
     2   You should have your feet flat on the floor.
     3   Make sure your forearms and hands are in a straight line.
     4   Your lower back should be supported.
     5   Your screen should be positioned to avoid reflected glare.
     6   Keep your shoulders relaxed.
     7   You should have your thighs tilted slightly.
     8   Make sure the top of the screen is at or slightly below eye level.

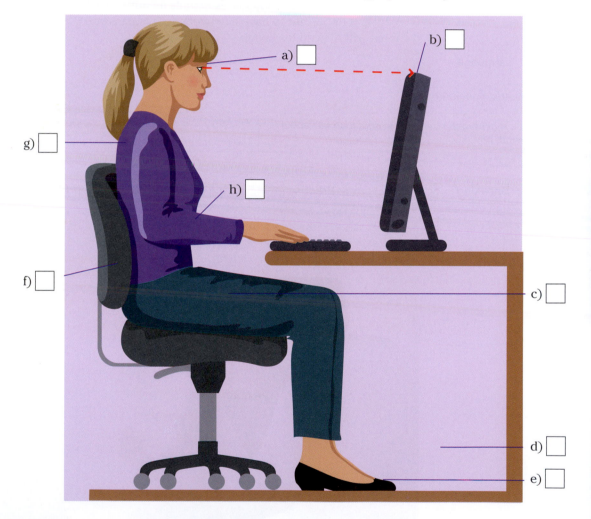

Speaking   **3**   Work in pairs. Answer these questions about the advice in 2.

     1   Do you always follow the advice?
     2   What other things can you recommend for good computer use?
     3   Have you had (or given) computer use training?

     4   Work in pairs. Practise giving instructions to each other.

     Example: Make sure you … .

Reading   **5**   Read this list of rules for using a company computer. Which ones do you follow? Why?

COMPUTER DOS AND DON'TS

Things you should do:
– Run Scandisk regularly to check and repair your file systems.
– Connect all peripherals before you switch the computer on.
– Keep your keyboard and screen clean.
– Keep CDs and DVDs in covers and hold them by the edge when using.
– Always shut down your laptop computer first if you need to move it.
– Secure your hardware from sudden power surges.

Things you should not do:
– Do not disconnect the keyboard, mouse, monitor, printer or any peripheral if the PC is on.
– Don't eat food or drink near the keyboard and computer. Don't blow smoke over your PC.
– Don't move or lift your desktop computer when it's on. Don't drop your laptop.
– Don't clean your hardware with a household polish or cleaner.
– Don't turn your computer off for lunch breaks.
– Don't load unauthorised software.

Vocabulary   **6**   Match the verb 1–5 with the noun a–e.

1 switch/turn off	a) software
2 eat	b) software
3 connect	c) peripherals
4 load	d) food
5 run	e) the computer

Speaking   **7**   Work in pairs. Discuss what other rules you can add to the two lists in 5. Compare your list with another pair.

8   What is the most important rule you can give about computer use? Work in pairs. Practise giving advice to each other.

Example: Always … ./You should … .

Security procedures

Speaking **1** What security procedures are you familiar with? Make a list and share it with the group.

Reading **2** Read this text on security and match the headings in the box with the paragraphs 1–5.

> Data transfer and backup   Email and network usage
> Password recommendations   Reporting IT security incidents
> Safety/security requirements

Systems and network security

All employees must follow security and safety procedures approved by the management.

1 _____

Only install and use software that the management has approved. Install the latest antivirus and antispyware tools.

Keep current with security software updates and patches.

Follow office health and safety standards.

2 _____

Choose a password that is difficult to guess: use between 6 and 8 characters, have letters in upper and lower case and intermix letters, numbers, and punctuation marks. Keep your password private. Change your password every 9 weeks.

3 _____

Configure your email software to use secure protocols. Use company official e-mail software only. Always double check that you are sending your message to the right recipient. Do not send sensitive data over the network. Use mail encryption to send sensitive data. Do not download unknown files or files for private use, such as movies and music.

4 _____

Transfer files via a secure connection. Back up files regularly on the server in your homefolder. Do not use external drives.

5 _____

Employees must notify their supervisor or IT help desk about any damage, misuse, irregularities or security breaches.

Vocabulary **3** Match the verb 1–6 with the noun a–f.

1	transfer	a) protocols
2	install	b) software
3	follow	c) procedures
4	use	d) files
5	notify	e) an incident
6	report	f) a supervisor

Speaking   **4**   What are the most important procedures to follow in the document in 2? Which procedures do people sometimes not follow?

Language

Expressing prohibition

a rule or requirement (We use these when it is necessary not to do this or to tell someone not to do something.)	You **mustn't** give your password to anyone.
	You **aren't allowed/permitted** to share your password with anyone.
a strong recommendation (We use this to give advice.)	You **shouldn't** use your date of birth in your password. (It is not a good idea to do this)

Listening   **5**   ▶ 🎧 49   Listen and repeat these sentences.

1   You mustn't put your cup of coffee on the computer.
2   You mustn't work without breaks.
3   You aren't allowed to smoke in the office.
4   We aren't allowed to send private emails.
5   You shouldn't eat lunch at your desk.

Speaking   **6**   Work in small groups. Talk about the computer regulations in your company or college. Use *you mustn't, you aren't allowed to* and *you shouldn't*.

Writing   **7**   Write a document listing the regulations you talked about in 7. Use these headings.

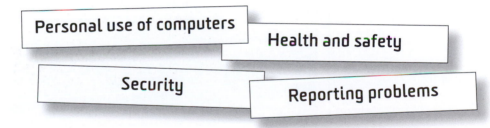

Personal use of computers

Health and safety

Security

Reporting problems

Reporting incidents

Speaking **1** Have you ever reported a security incident? What was it about?

Reading **2** Read these five IT incidents in a company.

A

Incident report

Date: 02.05

Report for: Miley O'Hara

Report prepared by: Ann Greshon

Incident: teacher, has accessed the database to change students's grade

Recommendations:

B

Incident: employee has changed the printer settings

Recommendations:

C

Incident report

Date:

Report for:

Report prepared by:

Incident: employee's children have installed games on company's laptop

Recommendations:

D

Incident: employee has downloaded a movie

Recommendations:

E

Incident report

Date:

Report for:

Report prepared by:

Incident: employee has installed P2P software

Recommendations:

Speaking **3** Work in pairs. Grade the incidents: 1 = the least serious. 5 = the most serious. Then compare your grades in small groups.

Writing **4** Write a short report to the IT supervisor on the most serious incident. You will need to give recommendations on how to deal with the incident.

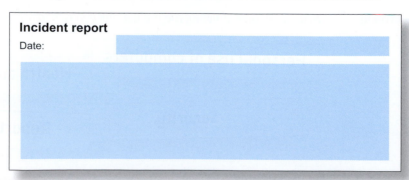

Incident report

Date:

Business matters

Reading **1** Work in pairs. You are systems safety coordinators. You have already completed two inspections of the IT systems in QuickFix Ltd. The first inspection was about network security and the second about health and safety in a workplace. Your investigation shows that the company has very poor security and safety systems. Look at the pictures and make notes.

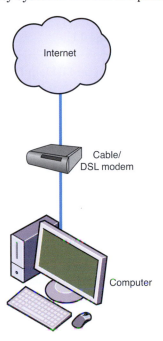

Speaking **2** Based on the information in the pictures and your notes, present your report after the inspections. Student A: talk about health and safety in the workplace. Student B: talk about network security.

1 Working in the IT industry

Business matters   **Speaking exercise 4 page 11**

> Student A: You work as an IT Help Desk Coordinator (Mrs Mahmoud). You receive an e-mail from a new employee. Call Sharifa. Tell her when her training is and answer her questions.

3 Websites

Website analytics   **Speaking exercise 8 page 23**

> Student A: Give Student B information about website traffic to your company's website. Ask about his or her website.
>
> Your company:
>
> _____
>
> Number of visitors: 2 million each year
>
> Visitor location: East Asia, Australia and New Zealand
>
> Length of time on site: 10 minutes

6 Network systems

Business matters   **Speaking exercise 4 page 51**

Student A	
Wednesday	morning – worked at home afternoon – went to the dentist
Thursday	morning – went to a company to check their network afternoon – installed network security at the company

7 IT support

Fault diagnosis   **Speaking exercise 8 page 53**

Student A

1   Call the IT help desk.
    You cannot access mail server.
    Ask for help.
    You changed your password last week.

Student A

2   Help Student B with the problem.
    At the moment the Internet connection
    is down.
    Try again later.

Student A

3   Call the IT help desk.
    You can't print out on network.
    Ask for help.

Student A

4   Help Student B with the problem.
    Change screen resolution?

Audio script

UNIT 1 Working in the IT industry

▶ 🌐 2

[N = Natasha; K = Khalid]
1   N: Hi, my name's Natasha.
    K: Pleased to meet you. I'm Khalid Ali.
    N: Pleased to meet you, too.
[P = Phillip; A = Ahmed]
2   P: Good morning. What's your name?
    A: I'm Ahmed. And you are?
    P: My name's Philip. Nice to meet you.
[T = Tim; A = All; I = Ingrid; L = Linda]
3   T: Hi everybody, this is Ingrid.
    A: Hi!
    T: Ingrid, this is Ahmed, Linda, Mohammed
       and Mansoor.
    I: Nice meeting you all.
    L: Likewise.
    T: Welcome to the team and good luck.

▶ 🌐 3

[Ka = Kathryn; K = Karim]
Ka: Karim, what do you do?
K: I'm a network administrator. Who do you
     work for?
Ka: I work for CISCO. I'm a system analyst there.
     Where are you from, Karim?
K: I'm from Kuwait. I work for Microsoft there.
     And where are you from, Kathryn?
Ka: I'm from the UK but now I live in Qatar. Do
     you know where Glenda's from?
K: She's from the US.
Ka: And what's her job?
K: She works for IBM. Her job is to set up new
     systems.

▶ 🌐 4

I'm, You're, She's, He's, It's, We're, They're

▶ 🌐 5

1   Hi, I'm Karl. I'm a software developer. I design
    and develop computer games. Thank you.
2   Good afternoon everyone, I'm Heba. I'm a
    system analyst. I solve computer problems.
    Nice to meet you all.
3   Hi, My name's Wojtek. I'm a database
    administrator. I analyse and present data.
    Thank you.

▶ 🌐 6

[A = Ahmed; B = Betty; M = Milo]
A: Where do you work, Betty?
B: I work for Dell in Dubai. What about you?
A: I work for HP in Budapest. What do you do,
     Milo?
M: I'm a software developer. I work for
     Microsoft in Prague.
B: Milo, do you know Frida?
M: Yes, I do. What do you want to know?
B: Where does she work?
M: She works with me in Prague. She designs
     websites for E-commerce.
A: I see. Right, let's go. The workshop starts in
     five minutes.

▶ 🌐 7

1   Where do you work?
2   What about you?
3   What do you do?
4   What do you want to know?
5   Where does she work?

▶ 8

[P = Penelope; D = Don]
P: Hi, Don. How are you?
D: I'm fine, thanks, Penelope. And you?
P: I'm OK. Bit tired from the flight.
D: Right.
P: What workshop do you want to attend today, Don?
D: I want to go to the CISCO network security workshop.
P: Sounds interesting. What time does it start?
D: It starts at 9.15.
P: And when does it finish?
D: It finishes at 4.00 in the afternoon.
P: Well, I want to attend the Microsoft Windows Applications workshop. It begins at 8.30 am and ends at 6.00 pm. But they have two breaks, at 10.30 and 12.45.
D: That's good.
P: Hope you enjoy your session.
D: You too. See you around.

▶ 9

1 7.05
2 6.45
3 8 o'clock
4 10.45
5 4.35
6 2.15
7 12 o'clock
8 9.50

▶ 10

1 It finishes at 5.00.
2 It ends at 8.00.
3 It starts at 6.00.

▶ 11

[A = Andrei; B = Bob]
A: Bob, can you help me, please?
B: Sure.
A: I don't understand this acronym. What does it stand for?
B: Let me see. W3. I'm not sure. Maybe WWW, the World Wide Web.
A: OK. What does P2P stand for?
B: It stands for person-to-person.
A: OK. What does IP mean?
B: It means Internet Protocol.
A: How do you spell 'Protocol'?
B: p – r – o – t – o – c – o – l.
A: Thanks.
B: You're welcome.

▶ 12

a h j k
b c d e g p t v z
f l m n s x z
i y
o
q u w
r

UNIT 2 Computer systems

▶ 13

[B = Bob; D = Daisy]
B: What do you think? Which laptop is better for the sales team?
D: I'm not sure. This computer has a bigger memory and I think it has a better processor.
B: And the other one?
D: Well, it is smaller.
B: And lighter.
D: Yes, you're right. Lighter and smaller.
B: But the bigger one is cheaper.
D: So what is our decision?
B: I'm not sure. Let's go for a coffee and discuss this again.

14

1 lighter
2 more efficient
3 longer
4 wider
5 heavier
6 faster
7 darker
8 softer
9 harder
10 more durable

15

[T = Tim; S = Simone]

T: What do you think about these three photo imaging packages?
S: It's a difficult choice. All three are very good but they have different strengths.
T: I agree.
S: Serif Image Plus has the best image correction.
T: OK.
S: But Magic Extreme has the fastest processing of images.
T: You're right. Also, Serif has the best special effects. But what about Snap Pro?
S: Well, it has the best dubbing options.
T: And Snap Pro is the best for burning photos.
S: I'm not sure. Serif has the most efficient compression.
T: Which is the most expensive?
S: Oh, Serif Image Plus.
T: And the cheapest?
S: Snap Pro.
T: Let's get Snap Pro then.
S: I'm still not sure!

16

1 We've got the best software.
2 Does it have the most reliable anti-virus software?
3 She has the cheapest computer.
4 They haven't got the latest version.
5 Do you have the fastest processor?
6 Has it got Windows?
7 They have the latest software.
8 It has the biggest screen.

17

[P = Paul; B = Brinitha]

P: Hi, Brinitha.
B: Hi, Paul.
P: How's it going?
B: Fine, fine.
P: What are you doing at the moment?
B: Oh, I'm installing Nero.
P: How are you getting on?
B: Well, I'm setting up a network. I'm using Microsoft Server.
P: Right. Where is Jackie today? Do you know?
B: Yes. She is on a training course today. She's learning about the new database system.
P: What about Mary and Imran? Where are they?
B: They aren't coming in today. They have a day off.

18

1 What are you doing now?
2 Are they setting up the network?
3 She's working at home today.
4 I'm not installing the software.
5 We're not using Word.

UNIT 3 Websites

19

1 Which websites do you use?
2 Why do you use Wikipedia?
3 What do you use CNN for?
4 When does she use CNN?

20

[S = Sarah; G = George]

S: George, I need some information about our website.
G: OK, what do you need to know?
S: Well, I need some information about website traffic, you know, external visits to our website.
G: OK.
S: Could you do a report for me?
G: Sure. When do you need it by?
S: Er, tomorrow morning, I'm afraid. It's for the finance director.
G: OK, what do you need to know exactly?
S: Well, the number of visitors to our website last month, their movements and actions on the website, and where they're from.
G: OK, I can do that.
S: Thanks very much indeed.

▶ 🔊 21

1 How many people visit the site?
2 Where do they go on the website?
3 How long do they spend on the website?

▶ 🔊 22

1 30,000
2 700,000
3 10,000,000
4 100,000
5 80,000

UNIT 4 Databases

▶ 🔊 23

[C = Chris; T = Tim]
C: Tim, could you help me a moment, please?
T: Sure. What's the problem?
C: I need some information about a book budget from the database.
T: OK.
C: But I don't know how to get it.
T: No problem.
C: So what do I do first?
T: Enter your name and password and press enter.
C: Erm … ?
T: You have got a password?
C: Erm, I can't remember it.
T: Use mine. Type in t evans, that's t – e – v – a – n – s, then snavet s – n – a – v – e – t.
C: OK.
T: Now press Enter. Now what is the name of the book?
C: *Basic French.*
T: OK. Type in that in the title field in the first column. Now Press Find. There it is. OK, budget. Click on Publishing and scroll down to Plant Costs and click on that.
C: Good. There's the budget in the second row. Thanks, Tim.
T: No problem.

▶ 🔊 24

1 Could you help me please?
2 Please could you help me?
3 Would you help me with this software?
4 Please could you explain how to do that?
5 Please would you give me your password?

▶ 🔊 25

[I = IT expert; C = Colleague]
I: Right, the first step in the process is you gather the raw data which you want to process. That's called collection. OK?
C: Yes, data collection.
I: Good. The second step is you create categories to organise the data into relevant groups. We call that sorting. Understood?
C: Sorting, right.
I: Then we arrange and systemise the data. That's coding. Got that?
C: Yes, I think so. The third step is coding.
I: After that, we enter the data into a system. That's entry.
C: OK.
I: Then, we clean the data and double-check for faults and inconsistencies. That's the validation part of the process.
C: Fine. Validation.
I: Finally we format and arrange the data so that it can be analysed. That's tabulation. All right?
C: Thanks very much.
I: No problem.

▶ 🔊 26

1 entry
2 collection
3 tabulation
4 validation
5 sorting
6 coding
7 gather
8 create
9 arrange
10 enter
11 double-check
12 format

▶ 🔊 27

1 emerging technology
2 cloud computing
3 data storage
4 hard drive
5 external drives
6 back-up providers

28

[T = Tim; S = Sandy]

T: Sandy, could you give me some advice on storage devices?

S: Sure. How can I help?

T: I'm a bit worried about my computer at home.

S: Right.

T: I've got lots of music and photos on my computer and I think I should back them up.

S: I know what you mean.

T: What should I buy?

S: I'd recommend an external hard drive. That's what I've got at home. How much can you spend?

T: $200.

S: That should be fine. You should be able to get something good for that. Oh, one thing: I'd really recommend you get one that backs up automatically from your computer when it is connected.

UNIT 5 E-commerce

29

[I = Interviewer; D = David]

I: David, tell me, how much of your business is online now?

D: Not much, really. Only about 7%.

I: Why's that, do you think?

D: Well, most of our customers buy our cleaning products in supermarkets when they buy their food. And most people go out to buy their food. They go to the supermarket.

I: Do you think this will change?

D: Probably but slowly. Last year our online buying was about 5% of our business.

I: So, it is growing a little.

D: Yes, but only a little. And in future our customers will still buy our products from the supermarkets on their websites. I don't think they will buy online from us direct.

30

1 not a lot of time
2 too much work
3 only a little money
4 a few computers
5 a lot of memory

31

1 open an account
2 go to the check-out
3 put an item in the basket
4 browse the website
5 choose an item
6 check the order

32

1 The company won't provide Internet access to all employees.
2 I'll do the security checks and then upgrade this week.
3 When will you finish the work?
4 Yes, I will.
5 No, she won't.

33

[M = Monika; S = Shayan]

M: Shayan, can you explain how a customer completes an online transaction?

S: OK, it's very easy. First, the customer will place an order. The seller's web server will confirm availability of the product and send a response. After that, the customer checks out and completes the payment instructions. Then the server will send a payment request to a payment gateway. The payment gateway will check the buyer's ability to pay with the bank. OK?

M: Fine. Go on.

S: The bank will respond and send payment acceptance or rejection to the seller's web server through the payment gateway. Finally, the customer will receive the server response with the order confirmation or rejection.

M: Will the customer have to register?

S: Yes, all buyers must have their accounts before they complete the transaction.

M: Thank you. Now I understand.

UNIT 6 Network systems

▶ 34

[A = Agatha; K = Katharina]

A: Hi, Katharina. It's good to see you again. How are you?

K: I'm fine. And you?

A: Fine, thanks.

K: I'm really glad to hear about your success.

A: Thank you.

K: So how can I help you?

A: I wanted to see you because I need your advice. We think we should offer our products and services online to increase our market share. What do you think?

K: That's a great idea. You should definitely do that.

A: Good. So what exactly should I do?

K: I'd recommend that you set up an E-commerce flower shop.

A: OK.

K: I'll send you an e-mail with some recommendations.

A: Oh, thank you very much. We ought to be ready for Mother's Day.

K: In that case, I'd suggest we start right away. Let me ask you some questions …

▶ 35

1 modem
2 repeater
3 bridge
4 router
5 gateway
6 switch
7 hub
8 wireless
9 access point
10 network connectors
11 network interface card

▶ 36

[B = Boris; A = Ahsan]

B: I have a problem with the network download speed. What can you suggest?

A: Why don't you change the hub?

B: I don't think that will work. The hub is fine.

A: OK. How about adding a repeater then?

B: Hmm, I'm not sure it will help. It's not a problem with the signal strength.

A: OK, then you should check the cables and network devices to make sure that they are compatible with your network.

B: What about changing the modem?

A: I don't think it's necessary. I think it's a problem with the bridge, switch or the router. You should look at the specifications.

B: OK, I will. Thanks for your help.

A: Why don't you check user recommendations on the internet as well?

B: Good idea. I'll do that.

▶ 37

1 Why don't you change the modem?
2 How about connecting a repeater?
3 What about looking on the website?

▶ 38

1 When did they start work?
2 They installed the computers yesterday.
3 We didn't work last week.
4 She went to the office on Sunday.
5 Did you finish the report?

▶ 39

[K = Karoline; S = Sam]

K: How do you describe network speed?

S: In bits, kilobits, megabits and gigabits. They describe network speed. For example, dial-up connections allow 56 kilobits per second and DSL from 512 kilobits per second to 3 megabits per second.

K: OK. I've got that. What about the range?

S: Range is the distance of network coverage, so distance units represent network range. Most countries use metric but some use feet as units of measurement. Metres or feet usually describe the range of a network. Home networking routers support a range up to 150 feet or 46 metres indoors and 300 feet or 92 metres outdoors.

K: Thanks.

40

1 77 kilobits per second
2 5 megabytes a second
3 2 gigabytes per minute
4 250 metres
5 40 feet

UNIT 7 IT support

41

[H = Haider; M = Maryam]

H: Hello, IT Help Desk.
M: Hi, this is Maryam from Human Resources.
H: Hi, this is Haider. How can I help you, Maryam?
M: I switched my computer off yesterday and today I can't turn it on.
H: What type of computer do you have?
M: I'm not sure. It's a desktop computer. It worked fine yesterday.
H: Don't worry. Have you checked the cable connections?
M: No, I haven't. I can see some cables but I don't know which cable goes where.
H: Make sure all cables are tight and fully plugged in.
M: Ok, give me a sec. Oh, I think I've found the problem. I have one cable that is unplugged. It's the power cable. Where does it go?
H: The power cable should go in the three-pronged port on the computer.
M: OK, done. Let me try now. It's working fine. Sorry about that. Stupid of me.
H: Maybe the cleaners disconnected your PC by mistake last night.
M: Maybe. Good, we've solved the problem. Thank you, Haider.
H: You're welcome. Have a good day.
M: You too.

42

1 checked
2 switched
3 unplugged
4 worked
5 disconnected

43

1 Have you run the computer in the battery mode?
2 How long have you had the iPad?
3 Have you charged the battery?
4 Has he opened the file?
5 Has she entered her username and password?
6 Have they changed the Internet Service Provider?
7 Have you checked the remaining disk space?
8 Have you installed or uninstalled software recently?
9 Has Dillip updated the drivers recently?

44

Customer 1
Today is 5 May. Please leave your message after the tone.
Hi. My name is Bolek. I've received a Word File but it won't open in Office. Can you help?
My contact number is 050 444 5553. Thank you.
Thank you for your call. The service person is Alex.

Customer 2
Today is 16 June. Please leave your message after the tone.
Hi, my name is Sara. I've lost a file that I opened from an attachment. Please help.
My contact number is 055 8214328. Thank you.
Thank you for your call. The service person is James.

Customer 3
Today is 13 July. Please leave your message after the tone.
Hello, my name is Sylvia. I've deleted some files. Can I recover them?
My contact number is 050 7895421. Thank you.
Thank you for your call. The service person is Mahmoud.

45

1 reversible ratchet driver
2 screwdriver
3 hex key set
4 pliers
5 wire cutter
6 wire stripper
7 insertion/extraction clipper
8 three prong holder
9 tweezers
10 anti-static wrist strap

46

[H = Helpdesk technician; T = Tuka]

H: Hello, Aqhel speaking. How can I help you?
T: Hi, my name's Tuka. I've upgraded my computer to Windows 7 and now I can't find my personal files anywhere!
H: I see.
T: I've checked Windows 'help' and that didn't tell me anything. I need one file urgently.
H: I'm sure we can find your file. Don't worry.
T: Well, I hope so.
H: What Windows version did you have before?
T: Before I had Windows Vista.
H: OK. Is your computer on?
T: Yes, it is.
H: Good. Find *Windows.old* folder in your C drive.
T: I don't understand. How? I can't see it in Windows Explorer.
H: Please go to the search box, write *Windows.old* and click enter.
T: OK.
H: The *Windows.old* folder contains different folders. Your folders and files are in Documents and Settings. You should find the files there.
T: I'll do that.
H: I'll come down to your office if you still have a problem. Good luck.
T: Thanks.

47

1 How can I help you?
2 I see.
3 I'm sure we can find your file.
4 Please go to the search box …
5 Good luck.

UNIT 8 IT security and safety

48

[L = Ludek; A = Ales]

L: Ales, can you check my laptop? Nothing seems to work.
A: Hmm, what have you done this time? Wow! Your laptop is a mess.
L: Sorry about that. I'll clean it up.
A: Have you updated your antivirus software recently?
L: Yes, I have. I did it last week.
A: Well, that's good.
L: I'm afraid I may lose my project. I haven't backed it up.
A: Hmm. You might have spyware or some other malware on your computer. You should install a good spyware doctor program. An antivirus program may not catch everything.
L: OK, I'll do that.
A: And why don't you protect your WLAN access with a password? It's likely you will attract hackers and piggybackers and then you might lose a lot of work.
L: Fine, I'll do that.
A: I'll scan your system with my anti-spyware software now and see if there is a problem.
L: Thanks.

49

1 Your mustn't put your cup of coffee on the computer.
2 You mustn't work without breaks.
3 You aren't allowed to smoke in the office.
4 We aren't allowed to send private emails.
5 You shouldn't eat lunch at your desk.

1 Working in the IT industry

Business matters   **Speaking exercise 4 page 11**

> Student B: You are Sharifa. You will recieve a call from Mrs Mahmoud in answer to your email. Make sure she answers the questions in your email.

3 Websites

Website analytics   **Speaking exercise 8 page 23**

> Student B: Give Student A information about website traffic to your company's website. Ask about his or her website.
>
> Your company:
>
> _____
>
> Number of visitors: 500,000 each month
>
> Visitor location: the Middle East and North Africa
>
> Length of time on site: 2 minutes

6 Network systems

Business matters   **Speaking exercise 4 page 51**

Student B	
Monday	morning – attended a training course at the college afternoon – went to the doctor
Tuesday	morning – worked at home afternoon – was off

Pearson Education Limited
Edinburgh Gate
Harlow
Essex CM20 2JE
England

and Associated Companies throughout the world.

www.pearsonelt.com

First published 2011
Third impression 2013

ISBN: 978-1-4082-69961

Set in ITC Cheltenham Book

Printed in China
GCC/03

Design: Pearson Education

We are grateful to the following for permission to reproduce copyright material:

Screenshots
Screenshot on page 26 from http://www.nick.co.uk/, Nickelodeon UK - Marty Batten and Olivia Dickinson; Screenshot on page 38 from http://www.amazon.co.uk/Revision-Express-AS-Media-Studies/dp/1408206617/ref=sr_1_8?s=books&ie=UTF8&qid=1290418162&sr=1-8, © 2010 Amazon.com, Inc. or its affiliates. All rights reserved; Screenshot on page 39 from: B&Q homepage, http://www.diy.com/diy/jsp/?_requestid=72368, courtesy of diy.com. Screenshot on page 25 from http://www.ft.com/uk/markets, © The Financial Times Ltd.16.11.10

We would like to thank the following for their kind permission to reproduce their photographs:

(Key: b-bottom; c-centre; l-left; r-right; t-top)

Alamy Images: David Kilpatrick 23, Digifoto Green 46cr, ICP 46l, Johann Helgason 46br, Kumar Sriskandan 15, Mode Images Ltd 37bl, Paul Paladin 64, Science Photo Library 61; Copyright 2010 Thomson Reuters: EndNote® 31tc, Reference Manager® 31r; Corbis: 21, Deepak Buddhiraja / India Picture 19, Helen King 35, 59, JGI / Jamie Grill / Blend Images LLC 24, JLP / Jose L. Pelaez 8, Jose Luis Pelaez Inc / Blend Images LLC 30, Josef P. Willems 36l, Mario Anzuoni / Reuters 48t, moodboard 20, Steve Raymer 9, Yukmin / Asia Images 27; Fotolia.com: Candy Box Photo 48b; Getty Images: Chabruken 33, Piotr Sikora 36c; Microsoft Corporation: Used with permission from Microsoft 31l; Photolibrary.com: Alex Mare-Manton / Asia Images 4c, Ariel Skelley / Blend Images 34, Corbis 51l, Dave & Les Jacobs / Blend Images 51r, David Burton / Fresh Food Images 65, Fiona Jackson-Downes and Nick White / Cultura 52, GoGo Images 4r, Ingram Publishing 44; Rex Features: 4l, Action Press 36r, Jason Alden 53, OJO Images 16, Tony Kyriacou 14; Science Photo Library Ltd: 46tr; SuperStock: Blend Images 37br, Fotosearch 10.

Cover images: Front: iStockphoto: Konstantin Inozemtsev Background; Photolibrary.com: Juice Images / Ian Lishman r, Tetra Images c, Yang Liu l

All other images © Pearson Education

Every effort has been made to trace the copyright holders and we apologise in advance for any unintentional omissions. We would be pleased to insert the appropriate acknowledgement in any subsequent edition of this publication.

Picture Research by Kevin Brown

7 IT support

Fault diagnosis   **Speaking exercise 8 page 53**

Student B
1 Help Student A with the problem.
   The mail server asks for a username
   and password.
   Has Student A used the wrong password?

Student B
2 Call the IT help desk.
   You cannot access the Internet at the moment.
   Ask for help.

Student B
3 Help Student A with the problem.
   There is a new default printer.

Student B
4 Call the IT help desk.
   The opened page is too large for the screen.